# THE GERMAN EXPELLEES: VICTIMS IN WAR AND PEACE

*Also by Alfred-Maurice de Zayas*

**NEMESIS AT POTSDAM**
**THE WEHRMACHT WAR CRIMES BUREAU**

# THE GERMAN EXPELLEES: VICTIMS IN WAR AND PEACE

Alfred-Maurice de Zayas

Translated by
John A. Koehler

150th YEAR

**M**

MACMILLAN

Originally published as *Anmerkungen zur Vertreibung der Deutschen aus dem Osten*. © Verlag W. Kohlhammer GmbH 1986
English translation © Alfred-Maurice de Zayas 1993
Original German version translated by John A. Koehler

First published in Great Britain 1993 by
THE MACMILLAN PRESS LTD
Houndmills, Basingstoke, Hampshire RG21 2XS
and London
Companies and representatives
throughout the world

ISBN 0-333-60469-5

A catalogue record for this book is available
from the British Library.

Printed in the United States of America by Haddon Craftsmen, O'Neill Highway, Scranton, PA.

# CONTENTS

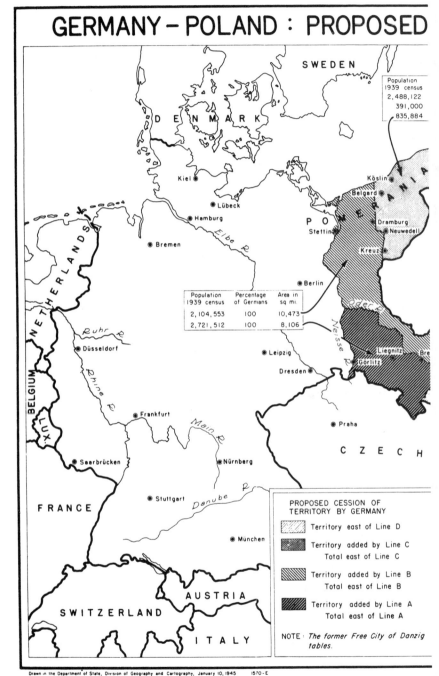

# GERMANY – POLAND : PROPOSED

SWEDEN

DENMARK

Kiel

Lübeck

Hamburg

Bremen

POMERANIA

Köslin

Belgard

Stettin

Dramburg

Neuwedell

Kreuz

Berlin

| Population 1939 census | | |
|---|---|---|
| 2,488,122 | | |
| 391,000 | | |
| 835,884 | | |

| Population 1939 census | Percentage of Germans | Area in sq mi. |
|---|---|---|
| 2,104,553 | 100 | 10,473 |
| 2,721,512 | 100 | 8,106 |

Düsseldorf

Leipzig

Dresden

Liegnitz

Görlitz

Bre

Ruhr R.

Rhine R.

Frankfurt

Main R.

Praha

CZECH

Saarbrücken

Nürnberg

FRANCE

Stuttgart

Danube R.

München

PROPOSED CESSION OF
TERRITORY BY GERMANY

Territory east of Line D

Territory added by Line C
Total east of Line C

Territory added by Line B
Total east of Line B

Territory added by Line A
Total east of Line A

NOTE: *The former Free City of Danzig*
*tables.*

AUSTRIA

SWITZERLAND

ITALY

NETHERLANDS

BELGIUM

LUX

Drawn in the Department of State, Division of Geography and Cartography, January 10, 1945    1570-E

# TERRITORIAL CHANGES

**LITHUANIA**

| Percentage of Germans | Area in sq. mi. |
|---|---|
| 93.8 (1925) | 14,282 |
| 92.8 (1923) | 754 |
| ca.99.0 (1925) | 6,812 |

● Memel

Area north of dotted line
Pop.: ca. 1,000,000
Area: 4,000 sq. miles

● Wilno

Gdynia
● Königsberg

DANZIG

**E A S T**

**P R U S S I A**

● Grodno

● Minsk

● Białystok

**U S S R**

Wista (Vistula) R.

● Warsaw

**WESTERN POLAND**

| Population 1931 census | Area in sq. mi. |
|---|---|
| 21,467,000 | 94,734 |

Łódź ●

● Brest Litovsk

**C U R Z O N — L I N E**

**EASTERN POLAND**

| Population 1931 census | Area in sq. mi. |
|---|---|
| 10,640,000 | 70,049 |

| Population 1939 census | Percentage of Germans | Area in sq. mi. |
|---|---|---|
| 1,527,491 | 57.0 (1914) | 3,750 |

slau

**UPPER SILESIA**

Beuthen ●
● Katowice
● Kraków

● Lwów

**S L O V A K I A**

● Cernăuți

**RUMANIA**

**HUNGARY**

| AREA IN SQ. MILES | POPULATION 1939 CENSUS |
|---|---|
| 18,032 | 4,015,613 |
| 6,812 | 835,884 |
| 24,844 | 4,851,497 |
| 10,473 | 2,104,553 |
| 35,317 | 6,956,050 |
| 8,106 | 2,721,512 |
| 43,423 | 9,677,562 |

*is not included in the above*

| PROPOSED ANNEXATIONS BY POLAND | AREA IN SQ. MILES | POPULATION 1939 CENSUS |
|---|---|---|
| | (Cumulative Totals) | |
| East of Line D | 14,766 | 3,406,613 |
| East of Line C | 21,578 | 4,242,497 |
| East of Line B | 32,051 | 6,347,050 |
| East of Line A | 40,157 | 9,068,562 |

NOTE: *Tables include Danzig and exclude East Prussia north of dotted line (probable minimum annexation by USSR).*

# FOREWORD

Many *Volksdeutsche* (ethnic Germans), who formerly lived between the Bohemian Forest and the Urals, the White and the Black seas, and who now inhabit contemporary Germany, Great Britain, and the Americas, are experts in what we call "ethnic cleansing." They obtained their specialized knowledge as victims of the ferocious reaction known as the Expulsion, which followed upon Adolf Hitler's genocidal imperialism. Because their mother tongue was German and Hitler's adopted fatherland was Germany, it has been difficult for those who fought or suffered under the Nazis to grant them much sympathy. Moreover, some among the *Volksdeutsche* were hell-bent to become junior partners in the Aryan master race and did all they could to deliver their communities as a fifth column for the Nazis.

Most of them, however, were indifferent to politics—farmers in East Prussia and the Romanian Banat, coal miners in Silesia. They were like ordinary people anywhere: not the actors, but the acted upon. As our neighbors and as citizens today, they share the opportunity to shape their destiny in free elections. In the 1930s, in Hungary or Poland, for example, their options were far more limited. The failure of the French, British, and Americans to support constitutional regimes in Spain in 1936 and in Czechoslovakia in 1938 left the political field open to communism and some form of fascism. This ultimately meant that the choice for anyone with an average amount of courage living in East-Central Europe was between Hitler and Stalin.

Contemporary Americans, safely and smugly hidden behind a Bill of Rights and a superpower military, might think that a choice between Hitler and Stalin was no choice at all. But that is because we have not been forced to make such choices. Not yet. For Danube Swabians in the Yugoslavian Batschka or German-Russians in the Ukraine, the choice usually came down to whom they hated more, Stalin or Hitler; which doctrine repulsed them more, communism or Nazism. Women and children, of course, were not consulted. The choices were made for them.

In most circumstances, any people who suffered the devastating casualties described by Dr. Alfred de Zayas in this volume and in his other works would logically be labeled as victims. Even if one were so bitter as to demand that the Germans should have provided their share of innocent victims, this condition was well met by the 15 million displaced and 2 million killed. To see none of the latter as innocent is to pose a concept of collective blood guilt that augurs poorly for the future. Yet such innocence has rarely been discussed outside of German-speaking countries. The taint of Nazism has been so severe that the German expellees have been victimized by both journalists and historians. Sinister motives for this phenomenon are unlikely. There has been not so much a concerted conspiracy to withhold the truth, as an embarrassed reluctance to tell it. The passions and confusions of World War II and the Cold War discouraged writers and politicians from defending a group of people who were as powerless as they were despised. *The German Expellees: Victims in War and Peace* should go a long way in righting this wrong.

Dr. de Zayas is well equipped, both professionally and academically, to remove the German expellees from the ranks of villains and place them among the victims; one might even say the last large group of Hitler's victims. Alfred de Zayas has been a human rights activist and has worked as a human rights expert for the past two decades, specializing in the rights of refugees and minorities. He has been sent on fact-finding missions to many countries and has examined *in loco* the human rights situation in numerous crisis areas.

There are dangers, of course, in a historian being as close to history in the making as de Zayas is. As respite from his legal work in Geneva he has been offered the dubious opportunity of viewing contemporary horrors firsthand. Such proximity to unfolding events brings the temptation to reach backward through history, to attempt to explain the past in terms of the present, instead of the other way around. Readers of *The German Expellees* need not worry. Alfred de Zayas's legal training at Harvard and his historical training at Göttingen (and Tübingen, where he was a Fulbright Graduate Fellow) have helped him to avoid the trap of understanding backward while forgetting that our predecessors could only live forward. His *Nemesis at Potsdam* systematically analyzed the Allied responsibility for the decisions to expel the Germans. His *Wehrmacht War Crimes Bureau, 1939-1945* has established beyond a reasonable doubt that a war crime is a war crime is a war crime, whether committed by German, Soviet, British, or American forces.

*The German Expellees* is a departure from Alfred de Zayas's other work only in its emphasis, not in its scholarly thoroughness or remarkable objectivity. What emerges here is a picture of who the German expellees were and where and when they settled in central and eastern Europe. We find among them poets and philosophers, farmers and businessmen; people whose talents were not only valued in German culture but were sought after by the

Habsburg emperors, Hungarian nobility, and Tsars Catherine the Great and Alexander I.

We discover also that they form major ripples among the waves of German emigration to the United States, Canada, and South America. In the new world, as in the old, their contributions have been aesthetic as well as mundane. Furthermore, the phenomenon of the West German economic "miracle" of the 1950s is inexplicable without the inclusion of the highly skilled labor force represented by the expellees.

Alfred de Zayas has, in effect, revealed the German expellees as human beings. He restores to them a humanity that was literally taken away from them by Hitler, Stalin, and the Allies and then figuratively withheld by historians and journalists, unwilling or unable to view that part of the 20th century as, in von Ranke's phrase, "it actually was."

As for any lessons concerning war crimes and crimes against humanity, a simple, powerful message emerges from this book and the entire body of Alfred de Zayas's scholarship and professional activity. If the peoples of the earth would really seek to diminish the horrors of mass murder, they might do better to concentrate less on loving their neighbors and more on simply not hating them. Once enough of us decided to change from love/hate to tolerance, our politicians would have no choice but to obey us.

*Charles M. Barber*
Professor of History
Northeastern Illinois University

# ACKNOWLEDGMENTS

I wish to thank the many people who by their knowledge and advice assisted with my research, thus making this book possible, among them contemporary political and diplomatic figures, surviving expellees and their descendants and the many helpful archivists in Germany, France, Great Britain, Belgium, Switzerland and the United States. I owe special thanks to my American translator John Koehler, who knew exactly what I wanted to say, and to my Dutch friends Wieneke and Walter Rabus, at whose summer home in the Auvergne, France, I finished rewriting the English manuscript. I also wish to thank Robert Conquest for giving permission to reproduce from his translation of *Prussian Nights*.

As representatives of the many others who accompanied me on my journey through this book, Dr. Walter Vorbach and his wife, Helene, deserve special mention as Sudeten Germans who found a new life in Heidelberg.

*Alfred-Maurice de Zayas,*
Lafont-Cassanieuze,
August 1992

# INTRODUCTION

The new world order that is emerging in the aftermath of the collapse of Marxist-Leninist systems throughout the world, the independence of former Soviet republics, the reunification of Germany, the secession of Slovakia from Czechoslovakia and the split-up of Yugoslavia calls for new strategies and new answers.

Europe is in flux. In this new world order the United States will be a major player, but not the only one, since it will be sharing with its former World War II enemies—Germany and Japan—responsibility for the welfare of the rest of the world.

After the fall of the Berlin Wall, a reunified Germany is on its way to becoming the leader of the new Europe. A functioning parliamentary democracy with 80 million souls and a powerful economy, Germany may well develop into America's most important partner. This is reason enough to acquaint ourselves not only with Germany's present but also with its history, both good and bad, and in particular with certain open questions that, although apparently dormant today, may eventually require answers.

Americans have further reason to learn more about German history, considering that so many Germans, Austrians and Swiss-Germans emigrated to the United States that it is estimated that at least one-fifth of all Americans have German ancestry. Indeed, in the nineteenth and early twentieth centuries, millions of immigrants came from the various German states and principalities, from the Austro-Hungarian Empire and other German-speaking areas of the old Europe, including East Prussia, Pomerania, East Brandenburg, Silesia, Bohemia, Moravia, Slovenia, Croatia, Serbia and Transylvania. It is from these areas that 15 million Germans were expelled at the end of World War II. Tens of thousands of these expellees eventually migrated to the United States and Canada, especially in the late 1940s and early 1950s.[1]

Few in the English-speaking world, even history buffs, know that, partly as a result of the Potsdam Conference of July-August 1945, millions of Germans lost their 700-year-old homelands in the eastern provinces of Germany and Eastern Europe. The expulsion of Germans from the East, a process that over 2 million did not survive, deserves our attention because of its implications for Europe and for ourselves. The expulsion and its attendant horrors are not overwrought fantasies of German revisionist historians. These events represent a historical episode of considerable consequence, and to understand post–World War II German history up to and following reunification, we must grasp it.

Even though nearly half a century has elapsed, we are still a long way from coping with this event, from a larger, representative overview; a long way from placing it within the context of twentieth-century German and European history and thereby granting it proper historical importance. Occasionally one gets an impression that the expulsion never happened, or that the issue is dead and buried as far as public awareness is concerned, especially when we hear and read the euphemistic terminology used to describe the events in eastern Germany in 1945. When mentioned at all in the press, these events are described as a "transference" or "displacement" of persons, as if they had simply taken a train ride west. Nor did the millions of ordinary people in East Prussia or Silesia who were violently forced to leave their homelands in the spring and summer of 1945 regard their fate as a "liberation." A historian who does not turn a blind eye to the human factors within historical events will not be able to ignore this tragedy without purposely downplaying or belittling its significance.

The immeasurable suffering borne by millions of refugees and expellees, by the more than 2 million who either perished as a result of their tribulations or were murdered in the process, by the more than 2 million later emigrants and finally by those who stayed behind, surviving as a dispersed minority in Eastern Europe—these agonies provide a wealth of material for scores of books, scholarly monographs, novels, poems; for documentary films and even plays. Gradually books are being written and films made, attempting to describe to an unwitting public the impact of this upheaval. Yet the twentieth century has witnessed many more horrors: the Armenian genocide, the Soviet gulags, the Nazi Holocaust against the European Jews, atomic bombs droppped on Hiroshima and Nagasaki, the Khmer Rouge atrocities in Cambodia, the rape of Kuwait, "ethnic cleansing" in the former Yugoslavia. One can but agree with the succinct appraisal by that great Silesian Nobel Laureate, Gerhart Hauptmann, who himself had to witness the expulsions of 1945-46: "World history has hit the skids."

Humankind must find ways to deal with its history. Each generation must take a new look at the past and come to grips with it, define its own parameters.

During World War II people just like us were responsible for great injustice and endless suffering: 50 million men, women and children died in this fratricidal conflict. Since that time, two generations of Americans, Belarusians, Britons, Croats, Czechs, French, Germans, Hungarians, Italians, Poles, Russians, Serbs,

Slovaks, Slovenes and Ukrainians have come along, their knowledge of the period dependent on accounts told by their elders, on book descriptions or distorted movie melodramas. Is there a scapegoat, a collective guilt for these calamities? No! Collective guilt is a non-historical, inhuman and unreasonable concept. There is, however, a collective morality to which we must all subscribe.

All victims of injustice deserve our respect. The crimes committed by the Nazis and Soviets against the Poles in the years 1939 to 1945 move us to existential identification with them. The merciless revenge that poured over the entire German civilian popultion of Eastern Europe, in particular in those sad years of the expulsions from 1945 to 1948 should also awaken compassion, for in either case the common people—farmers and industrial workers, the rich and the poor—all were the victims of politics and of politicians. In judging these events, the nationality of a victim must not matter; pain and suffering have no nationality. Nor does murder. Every crime is reprehensible, regardless of the nationality of its victim—or of the victimizer.

This book does not attempt to present a complete history of the expulsion tragedy. It provides a retrospective accompanied by eyewitness accounts of survivors of the expulsions, thereby lending immediacy and reality to the character and extent of this European calamity. The style of each eyewitness account is preserved; their selection and the running commentaries appended thereto are the work of a nonparticipant, an American of the postwar generation who, having lived in Germany as a Fulbright Fellow, was overwhelmed by this story. The presentation contained within these pages illustrates the many different ways in which this event affected so many lives. Shortsighted political decisions tore people away from their ancestral roots, from a way of life generations old; these decisions also brought death and destruction to many. Some of these testimonies, including those of the diplomats and politicians involved, were collected by a number of historians, among them the author of this book, for a prime-time television special broadcast in Germany in 1981, making use of original footage from the *Deutsche Wochenschau* and from the U.S. Army Signal Corps, which captured for posterity important documents on the expulsion. Some of these films are stored at the U.S. Army archives in Tobyhanna, Pennsylvania.

The first draft of this book emerged directly from the author's script for the television documentary, upon request by the German publisher, but was significantly improved and completed for the three German editions hitherto published, and again revised and updated by the author for the American edition.

The historical ramifications of the expulsions can hardly be overestimated, for the facts clearly show that a peaceful ethnic coexistence, indeed a mutually beneficial ethnic cooperation, thrived in these regions for hundreds of years, back to the twelfth century. It was all brought to a violent end. Perhaps after the demise of Communism, and with it of the East-West confrontation, a new economic and cultural exchange will emerge in Central and Eastern Europe, enabling all citizens of the region to achieve their human rights. The Helsinki process, engendered by the Conference on Security and Cooperation in Europe, has already made considerable progress in this direction.

May this book generate interest in this hitherto ignored tragedy and lead to a new respect for these forgotten victims and to more compassion and understanding for our neighbors.

1. The War: The Russian sign reads: "Soldiers! Majdaneck does not forgive. Take revenge without mercy!", Goldnap, East Prussia, October 1944 (*Bundesarchiv*).

2. Under- and over-aged German recruits at a railroad station in East Prussia, 1944 (*Bundesarchiv*).

3. Massacred German civilians who did not flee Nemmersdorf, East Prussia before the arrival of the Soviet Army, October 1944 (*Bundesarchiv*).

4. The flight: long columns of covered wagons attempting to escape the war zone, East Prussia 1945 (*Bundesarchiv*).

5. Plundered possessions of would-be refugees after their trek was overtaken by the Soviet Army in East Prussia, October 1944 (*Bundesarchiv*).

6. Some 2 million Eastern Germans were evacuated by ship from Pomerania and, in this case, East Prussia (*Bundesarchiv*).

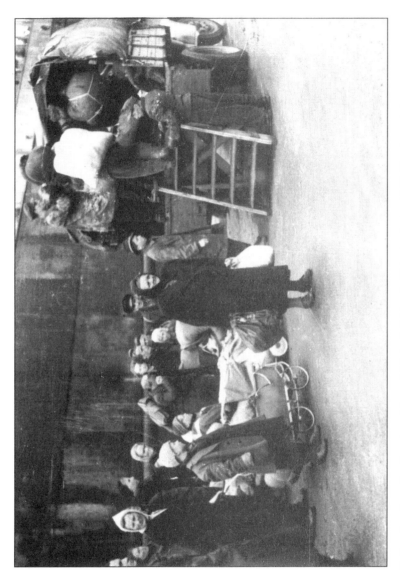

7. Expellees from East Prussia arriving at Meldorff, Schleswig-Holstein, Spring 1945 (*Bundesarchiv*).

8. Germans trekking westwards, summer 1945 (*Bundesarchiv*).

9. Expellees moving westwards through Brandenburg, summer 1945 (*US Army*).

10. German refugees, who had attempted to flee the advancing Soviet Army, being guarded by Russian soldiers, Volyne, Czechoslovakia, May 1945 (*US Army*).

11. Austrians and German refugees from Silesia who fled from the Soviet Army, waiting in Volyne, Czechoslovakia to be returned to the Russian lines, May 1945 (*US Army*).

12. Sudetenland Germans awaiting treatment from US Army medics, having been beaten and forced from their homes by Czechs, Pilsen, Czechoslovakia, May 1945 (US Army).

13. German expellees in Wurzen, Germany attempting to escape from the Russian Army to the American lines, April 1945 (*US Army*).

14. Two wagons containing all the possessions of a German family from Poznan, Poland stopping for repairs en route for resettlement in the Russian zone of Germany, February 1946 (*US Army*).

16. Expellees with their meagre possessions, no place, no date (*Presse- und Informationamt der Bundesregierung*).

Berlin, summer 1945 (Presse- und Informations...

17. Refugees from Pomerania in the ruins of Berlin, July 1945 (*National Archives*).

18. A Red Cross village built for German refugees (*Swiss Red Cross*).

19. In the hungry years, 1945-48, looking for food in garbage bins became a daily activity (*Swiss Red Cross*).

20. Ethnic Germans from the Danube basin, known as *Donauschwaben*. The *Donau-schwaben* suffered the greatest losses in the flight and expulsion (*Swiss Red Cross*).

21. *Donauschwaben* at a refugee camp in Bavaria (*Swiss Red Cross*).

22. Sudetenland Germans at a Munich refugee camp, November 1947 (*US Army*).

23. German refugees crossing the barbed wire between the Russian and British zones of occupation (*Swiss Red Cross*).

24. A Silesian expellee facing an uncertain future, 1948 (*Swiss Red Cross*).

# 1

# The Germans of
# East Central Europe

German expellees? Who are they? Expelled from where? And where do they and their descendants now live?

The German expellees from Central and Eastern Europe and two generations of their offspring live today in a diaspora, the world over, including the United States. The majority of them, however, reside in all 16 provinces (*Laender*) of what was formerly the German Democratic Republic and the Federal Republic of Germany, notably in Saxony, Brandenburg, Thuringia, Mecklenburg, Nordrhein-Westphalia, Bavaria, Lower Saxony and Baden-Wuerttemberg, over 14 million in all, or nearly 20% of the population of reunified Germany. Every fifth German has roots in the eastern provinces of prewar Germany, in the Sudetenland or in Southern and Eastern Europe.

Of course, the expellees and their descendants no longer live in closed communities, distinct from any other town or village in Germany. Instead they have become integrated within Germany, circulating among the native population as equals, for they are Germans like the rest. Though many still marry among their own, fully half of them have found their spouses among the local West German population.

East Prussians, Pomeranians and Silesians are especially prominent in Nordrhein-Westphalia; Sudeten Germans are prevalent in Bavaria, with Baden-Wuerttemberg the preferred new homeland for those originally from the former Soviet Union and the states of Southeast Europe. Smaller German *Laender* such as Schleswig-Holstein are home to many Pomeranians and Baltic Germans; the Rheinland-Palatinate, to many East Prussians; Saxony, to many Silesians and Sudeten Germans. Königsberg, Memel, Danzig, Stettin, Breslau, Oppeln, Karlsbad, Eger— these cities are forever bound to German history. In the provinces east of the frontier at the Oder-Neisse rivers as well as in the Sudetenland, Germans had lived and prospered for some 700 years. They founded cities, introduced German law, built the Hanseatic League, cultivated the land, developed industries and mines; they composed music, wrote poetry and prose, and philosophized.

The lands east of the Oder-Neisse were bountiful and beautiful, more sparsely settled than in the west, colder in winter, warmer in summer.

> This is the forest primeval. The murmuring pines and the
> hemlocks,
> Bearded with moss, and in garments green, indistinct in the
> twilight,
> Stand like Druids of eld, with voices sad and prophetic,
> Stand like harpers hoar, with beards that rest on their bosoms.
> Loud from its rocky caverns, the deep-voiced neighboring ocean
> Speaks, and in accents disconsolate answers the wail of the forest.
> This is the forest primeval; but where are the hearts that beneath it
> Leaped like the roe, when he hears in the woodland the voice of the
> huntsman?
> Where is the thatch-roofed village, the home of [the . . .] farmers,—
> Men whose lives glided on like rivers that water the woodlands,
> Darkened by shadows of earth, but reflecting an image of heaven?
> Waste are those pleasant farms, and the farmers forever departed!
> Scattered like dust and leaves, when the mighty blasts of October
> Seize them, and whirl them aloft, and sprinkle them far o'er
> the ocean. . . .[1]

A remembrance of East Prussia or Pomerania? Yes, it could well be. But it was with these words that the American poet Henry Wadsworth Longfellow immortalized the sadness and the desolation that ensued upon the inhuman expulsion of 15,000 French farmers from Nova Scotia in 1755. They had settled and lived there in peace for 100 years. The English governor, Charles Lawrence, wanted to be rid of these French Catholics, whom he considered potentially disloyal to the British crown. Their homes were confiscated, their families torn apart. The men were loaded in ships and dispersed among the other British colonies; wives and children were separated from their husbands and fathers, never to see each other again.

There have been many such expulsions in history. Recall the fate of Jews, expelled from Spain in 1492; the Huguenots of France, forced to flee in 1685 and again in 1701; the Salzburg Protestants, forced to abandon their homes, albeit in a less brutal fashion, in 1731-32. Oddly enough, it was precisely because of oppressive intolerance in other places that many of the persecuted found their way to new lives in Prussia. The Huguenots and Salzburgers who settled there became as Prussian as the natives. Two hundred years later they were again expelled.

But how did the greater masses of ethnic Germans come to be in Central and Eastern Europe, areas that today are part of Poland, the Czech and Slovak Republics, Hungary, Russia, Belarus, the Ukraine, Romania, Slovenia, Croatia and Serbia?

## GERMAN SETTLEMENT IN EAST CENTRAL EUROPE SINCE THE TWELFTH CENTURY

During the nineteenth century, German nationalists constantly pointed to the fact that Germanic tribes had been long settled in modern-day Poland—consider the Vandals, who in A.D. 400 under King Geiserich moved westward. The province of Silesia took its name from the Silinger tribe, before these people likewise headed west to settle finally along the Rhein and even in Andalusia, Spain. The lands along the Vistula River were settled by the Goths. Around A.D. 200 they began their migrations to the south, splitting into Ostrogoths, who ended up in the Crimea, Balkans and Italy; and the Visigoths, who settled in regions that later became France and Spain.

These are historical facts, but it is also true that the Ostrogoths and Visigoths cannot be regarded as direct forebears of modern Germans. While the eastern Germanic tribes had been settled for several hundred years in regions that comprise modern Poland, they nevertheless abandoned these settlements for the most part, yielding the lands to later influxes of Slavic tribes that settled as far west as the Oder and even the Elbe rivers. Around the year 960 the Kingdom of Poland came into existence under Mieszko I. At its heart lay the regions around the Warta River (Poznan and Gnesen), Lake Goplo and the central Vistula. The Piast Dynasty invited untold numbers of German monks, peasants, artisans and knights into the country from the twelfth through fourteenth centuries. The industry of these immigrants constituted a major contribution to the prosperity of the country. The settlement of Polish regions by Germans was voluntary and at the behest of Polish rulers. To speak of a German *Drang nach Osten* (Urge Eastward) betrays an anachronistic perspective and unfairly characterizes this largely peaceful settlement during the Middle Ages.

It was primarily the Cistercian Order that undertook the Christianization of Pomerania, where they established an Abbey at Buckow in the year 1260. Hand in hand with the monks came the farmers and the businessmen, who founded the hanseatic city of Stettin in 1243. Stargard was founded in 1253 and Kolberg in 1255.

Farther to the north lived non-Slavic peoples, among them the Pruzzens on the Baltic Sea. The Polish princes tried unsuccessfully to rule them. At the start of the thirteenth century Duke Konrad of Masovia asked the Teutonic Order, one of the spiritual orders of knights that arose during the Crusades, for support. The Hohenstaufen Kaiser Friedrich II responded with the issuance of the Golden Bull of Rimini in 1226, by which document he justified the conquest and Christianization of Prussian lands. His friend and adviser Hermann of Salza, Grand Master of the order, accepted Konrad's appeal and was invested by the kaiser with Prussia and the Kulmerland.

After the Pruzzens and other Baltic tribes as far as Estonia had been subjugated and converted to Christianity, the Teutonic Order consolidated its political power in a state that occupied the Baltics from Danzig to Reval Tallinn. The grand master's seat of authority was the Marienburg Castle on the Nogat River. German settlers founded 93 cities and 1,400 villages in Prussian lands east of the Vistula. They brought with them German law and established a prosperous nation. For 700 years they called this their homeland, a period longer than the entire history of an America colonized by Europeans.

German settlers moved into other regions of Central and Eastern Europe. King Ottokar II (1253-1278), among other sovereigns, promoted German settlements in Bohemia and Moravia. It was thus, 700 years ago, that a German-settled region near the Sudeten Mountains came into existence; only centuries later would it be called the Sudetenland. The westernmost corner of this territory, commonly known as the Egerland, was actually originally a part of the Duchy of Bavaria and not of the Kingdom of Bohemia. The city of Eger was a German mercantile center that, since the twelfth century, had belonged directly to the kaiser, and not to a count or lesser nobleman. Its castle served as an imperial palace for the Staufer kaisers. It was from this palace that in the year 1213 Kaiser Friedrich II proclaimed a Golden Bull for Pope Innocence III on the touchy issue of investiture of bishops in the Reich. Not until 1322 did Kaiser Ludwig the Bavarian pledge the Egerland to the Bohemian King John of Luxemburg. The population of the whole area remained ethnically and culturally German as before, even if formally the feudal allegiance shifted from German kaiser to Bohemian king.

Meanwhile the migration of German settlers toward the southeast continued, beyond the Carpathian Mountains to Moldavia and Walachia, as far as the Black Sea. The German settlements of Bessarabia to the north and Dobrudscha south of the Danube River delta developed. This colonization was characterized by the clearing of trees: The primeval forests of the Carpathian arc were opened up to permit the establishment of many cities and towns. In the mid-twelfth century the village of Hermannsdorf (later Hermannsstadt) was founded in Transylvania (called Siebenbuergen in German, because of the seven castles built) by peasants from Nuremberg. When, in the middle of the thirteenth century, the Mongols had overrun Russia and destroyed Hermannsdorf (1241), the Hungarian king Bela IV brought primarily German settlers to Siebenbuergen to protect his borders. In the seventeenth century Siebenbuergen became a province of the Habsburg monarchy.

The Buchenland, or Bukovina, was settled by Ruthenes, Romanians and Germans. In 1775 this region also came under Habsburg control as a more or less independent crown province.

Among the Germans in southeastern Europe, it is the 1.5 million Danube Swabians, or *Donauschwaben,* who make up the largest group. These settlers came initially from lands bordering on the west, later from southern German regions on either side of the Rhein. They settled in the Hungarian basin and regions that later became Romania and Yugoslavia. After Hungary had been freed of Turkish rule, these Germans followed the clarion call of the kaiser to resettle lands left barren and abandoned by the invaders. A law to this effect was decreed in 1689, but the larger immigration of German farmers and peasants did not really begin until after 1723. The areas settled by the "Schwaben," as all who came were called regardless of their actual origin (from the Rhein-Palatinate, Hessen, etc.), were dispersed throughout the Hungarian plains. Focal points were the lands around Budapest— the southwest Hungarian highlands where, in 1941, 11,000 residents claimed German as their ethnic origin and 22,300 German as their mother tongue; the *Schwaebische Tuerkei,* or Swabian Turkey, south of Lake Balaton; Slavonia between the Sava and Drava Rivers; and to the west of this province, Syrmia.

The Danube Swabians also settled in the Batschka, a region that lies between the Danube and Theiss rivers and extends into the former Yugoslavia. But it is the Banat region that became the most significant area of Swabian settlement, stretching east of the Theiss to the Danube and the Carpathians. Eighty-six exclusively German and 332 predominantly German communities were spread over Romanian, Yugoslavian and Hungarian territory. The Danube Swabians were a peaceful and industrious people, who loved the land that had welcomed them:

There in distant Hungary
Stands a village small and bright,
Embraced by murm'ring forests
And the blessings of prosperity.
At the village outskirts
A little cottage has been built,
Which, within its tiny rooms,
Guards all that stirs my heart.

—Nikolaus Lenau[2]


## CULTURAL ACHIEVEMENTS OF THE EASTERN GERMANS

What role did these eastern Germans play in German history? Which famous Germans came from their ranks?

Reich President Paul von Hindenburg (president 1925-34; field marshal during World War I) was born in Posen (Poznan) in 1841, when it was part of Prussia. Rocket scientist Wernher von Braun was also born there, in 1912. He subsequently emigrated to the United States, became an American citizen and helped put the first man on the moon.

The leader of the German Social Democratic party, Kurt Schumacher (1894-1952), was born in Kulm, West Prussia. Art historian Georg Dehio came from the Baltics, born in 1850 in Reval (Tallinn), Estonia. Among famous Danube Swabians are Nikolaus Lenau (pseudonym of Niembsch von Strehlenau), the romantic poet born in 1802 in Csatad, Hungary; and playwright and novelist Adam Mueller-Guttenbrunn, born in 1852 in the Banat.

The Sudetenland gave birth to Ferdinand Porsche, born in 1885 in Maffersdorf near Reichenberg (today Liberec), the builder of the first Volkswagen and later, developer of the sports car that bears his name. He too belongs to the expellees, settling in Stuttgart, where he died in 1951.

The naturalist and Augustinian monk Gregor Mendel was born in the Moravian town of Heinzendorf in 1822. He lived and worked in Bruenn (Brno), where he formulated his famous laws of genetics. It was there he died in 1884.

Artisans Rudolf and Leopold Blaschka came from Aicha, Bohemia. In their Dresden studio from 1877 to 1937 they created the world-famous glass flowers commissioned by Harvard University, more than 4,000 pieces of astonishing beauty, on display to this day in the Harvard Botanical Museum in Cambridge, Massachusetts.

Rainer Maria Rilke, one of the great German poets, was born in 1875 in Prague. The writer and peace activist Bertha von Suttner was born there as well in 1843. She attained world fame when she popularized the concept of peace at a time when honor and glory were associated with the martial arts. In 1905 she became the first woman to receive the Nobel Prize. Her most famous work is entitled *Die Waffen Nieder (Put Down Your Weapons)*.

A great many Jews, born in Bohemia and Moravia, were part of and contributed immortal works to the German cultural milieu. Franz Kafka was born in 1883 in Prague, as was Franz Werfel, the mouthpiece of the Expressionist movement, in 1890.

The great philosopher Edmund Husserl, professor at Goettingen and Freiburg im Breisgau, was born in 1859 in Prossnitz, Moravia, and became the founder of the School of Phenomenology; Sigmund Freud, founder of psychoanalysis, was born in 1856 in Freiburg, Moravia; and the superlative Romantic composer and conductor Gustav Mahler (1860-1911), was born in Kalischt, Bohemia, although he is historically inseparable from the city of Vienna, where he directed the State Opera during its pinnacle of fame, under the legendary reign of Kaiser Franz Josef, and where he died in 1911. He is buried in the Grinzing Cemetery.

During World War II, before the expulsion from the Sudetenland had begun, the distinguished Heldentenor Peter Hofmann was born in Marienbad on August 12, 1944, a man known to every opera aficionado not only as a great singer but also as a convincing actor. Recently he has launched a successful career as a rock singer.

Among the younger generations, many children of expellees have distinguished themselves. Since they are as German as any Bavarian or Westfalian, few would guess that they are of eastern German ancestry. Consider, for example, Boris Becker, German tennis champion and three-time Wimbledon winner. His mother Elvira, née Pisch, is a Moravian German from Kunewald, Neutitschein County, not far from Olmütz and Moravian Ostrau.

Well-known German musicians came from East Prussia, including Otto Nikolai, born in 1810 in Königsberg, whose operetta *The Merry Wives of Windsor* is known and heard throughout the world. And E. T. A. Hoffmann, writer and composer, was likewise born in Königsberg; he was one of the precursors of musical Romanticism. His writings also had an enduring effect on musical development in that they provided original material for, among others, Wagner's *Die Meistersinger von Nürnberg*, Tchaikovsky's ballet *The Nutcracker*, Leo Délibes' ballet *Coppelia* and, of course, Offenbach's opera *The Tales of Hoffmann*.

Any catalog of the fine arts must make mention of the etchings and sketches of Käthe Kollwitz (1867-1945) from Königsberg, known for her cycle based on

Gerhart Hauptmann's *The Weavers* and the series of wood engravings entitled *War*, originals of which can be admired at the Library of the League of Nations in Geneva. She also expressed her art in sculpture. Lovis Corinth, born in 1858 in Tapiau, is one of the best-known German painters, one of the leaders of Impressionism and certainly the most important German painter of his generation. Some of his portraits form part of the permanent exhibition of the Musee d'Orsay in Paris.

East Prussia is the homeland to numerous poets, such as Johann Gottfried Herder (1744-1803), and more recently, Agnes Miegel, born in 1876 in Königsberg. She experienced the expulsion firsthand and produced in 1949 a volume of refugee poems entitled *You Are Still Part of Me*:

> Once there was a land—how dearly did we love it—
> Yet waves of horror rolled over it, as dunes of sand.
> Vanished as the elk's trail in marsh and meadow
> Is every trace of man and beast.
> Frozen in the snow, consumed in the flames,
> Miserably they wasted in enemy hands.
> How deep they lie under the Baltic's waves,
> Their bones awash in bays and straits.
> They sleep upon Jutland's sandy bosom, —
> And we, the last of our kind, wander homeless,
> Strewn about like seaweed after the storm,
> Driven aimlessly like the autumn leaves, —
> Heavenly Father, You alone know our desolation![3]

Miegel died in Bad Salzuflen, Westfalia, in 1964.

In the realm of philosophy two names stand out: Immanuel Kant (1724-1804), from Königsberg, author of *The Critique of Pure Reason* (1781) and *The Critique of Practical Reason* (1788), in which he developed the idea of the categorical imperative; and Arthur Schopenhauer (1788-1860) from Danzig, the capital of West Prussia, author of *The World as Will and Idea* (1819).

Among Pomeranians we first think of the poet Ewald von Kleist from Koeslin (1759-1815) and of the natural scientist Karl August Dohrn, born in 1806 in Stettin, as well as his son, zoologist Anton Dohrn, born in the same city in 1840. Most prominently we celebrate the great Romantic painter Caspar David Friedrich, born 1774 in Greifswald, whose moody works evoke poetic images, intimate impressions captured with the brush. Our sense for the magnificence and eternity of Friedrich's art has grown especially in the years following World War II. Counted among his most famous works are *The Cross in the Mountains, The White Cliffs on the East Coast of Ruegen* and the powerful image of *The Monk by the Sea,* a most moving document of man's ineffable solitude, standing alone on the shore of a gray and infinite sea, gazing at the heavy, menacing clouds.

Among Silesians we remember atomic physicist and Nobel Prize winner Max Born, born in 1882 in Breslau of Jewish origin, who later emigrated to Edinburgh, Scotland, in 1936. Otto Klemperer, the famous Wagnerian conductor, was born in 1885 in Breslau. The outstanding Impressionist, later Expressionist painter (*Ich und die Stadt,* 1913) Ludwig Meidner, born 1884 in Breslau, emigrated to London in 1936 but returned to Germany after the war, where he died in 1966. The brilliant poet of the German baroque Andreas Gryphius was born in 1616 in Glogau.

Perhaps the most prominent Silesian poet of all time was Joseph Freiherr von Eichendorff (1788-1857), born in Lubowitz near Ratibor. Lyricist par excellence, his verses make part of German literary history and not just parochial Silesian homeland literature. The poem "Moonlit Night" was set to music by Robert Schumann; it is one of the most often sung classical *Lieder.* Perhaps even more beautiful is Eichendorff's *Im Abendrot* ("At Sunset"), chosen by composer Richard Strauss as the last of his exquisite cycle of *Four Last Songs* (1948):

Hand in hand we walked
Through joy and sorrow.
Now we rest from all these journeys,
Overlooking tranquil lands.
Valleys softly slope around us,
while the air is growing dark.
See the two larks climbing,
dreaming of the fragrance of the night.
Step closer, let them flutter;
soon shall be the hour of sleep,
lest our path we lose
in this solitude.
O Peace, so broad and still!.
Deep is the sunset's red,
How tired of walking are we—
could this perhaps be death?[4]

## GERHART HAUPTMANN IN AGNETENDORF

Eichendorff's fellow Silesian Gerhart Hauptmann (1862-1946) received the Nobel Prize for Literature in 1912. He was actively writing until shortly before his death. His despair for wartorn Germany was reflected in the four dramas of the *Atrides Tetralogy*, completed in 1945, when Germany had sunk into murder and chaos. The "fifth" drama in the tragedy was played out by life itself, the final line having been spoken by Soviet Colonel Sokolov, who, on April 7, 1946, handed Hauptmann at his home in Agnetendorf, Silesia, the deportation order drafted by the Polish government. At first, the Supreme Commander of the Soviet Forces, Marshal Georgi K. Zhukov, had offered the writer an opportunity to resettle in Dresden or Berlin, but Hauptmann refused, an act that created a sensation in Poland and in the West. However, the expulsion made no exceptions. Whether elderly or even Nobel Prize winner, the all-encompassing fate would not spare him.

"This time I come on official business," said Sokolov, who had already visited Hauptmann on several occasions. "I hereby convey to you the final offer of the Soviet Military Administration. The Germans in the county of Hirschberg will be completely evacuated. The Polish government is insistent. Even you, honored Herr Doktor, cannot remain any longer without placing yourself in jeopardy."[5]

"Well," said Hauptmann, "we shall have to go. . . ." He spoke in such a subdued monotone that the colonel could not understand him until Margarete Hauptmann repeated her husband's words. Interestingly, the colonel did not stipulate a time for their departure. Later the old man would cry out to his wife: "Gretchen, how can I abandon my Silesia?"

He fell ill. His fever worsened. In his death struggle he uttered his last words—in the form of a question. No artistic legacy, no appeal to the world, not even a word of affection for his deeply beloved wife, but rather a question still reflecting on his homeland: "Am I still in my own house?"[6] Thus he died, preempting the execution of deportation.

It was a disgrace that such a question was even asked; a question that astonishes for the very fact it had to be asked. Hauptmann died on June 6, 1946, at 3:10 P.M. It was his wish to be buried in the Wiesenstein Park beneath the crest of the Riesengebirge. But his body was instead transported to the Soviet Zone of Occupation where, on July 28, it was interred in the village of Kloster on Hiddensee Island near Stralsund.

How could this have happened, how could an internationally celebrated writer have been driven from his home? How did things get so far? In Europe, in the twentieth century?

The expulsion of Germans from their ancestral homelands belongs to the history of a war unleashed by Hitler, a war that eventually turned back upon Germany. The expulsion and its attendant horrors can only be imagined, indeed understood against the backdrop of unspeakable crimes committed by National Socialists in the East, in Auschwitz, Treblinka, Warsaw and Russia.

## EASTERN GERMANS WITHIN THE RESISTANCE

The Germans of the East were the ones who suffered most for the politics of Hitler, and doubly so. Before they were expelled from their eastern German homelands, a significant number of their leaders fell victim to Hitler. The German resistance to Hitler was essentially driven and directed by the Prussian nobility and the Prussian corps of officers. After the failed assassination attempt against Hitler on July 20, 1944, the responsible leaders were arrested and ultimately hanged. Among those executed were Erwin von Witzleben, born in Breslau; Ewald von Kleist-Schmenzin of Pomerania; Peter Yorck Graf von Wartenburg and Helmuth James Graf von Moltke, co-founders of the Kreisauer Circle in Silesia; theologian Dietrich Bonhoeffer of Breslau; and Carl Friedrich Goerdeler of Schneidemuehl, West Prussia, mayor of Königsberg, later lord mayor of Leipzig, and the person who had been selected by the conspirators to head the post-Hitler government.

These eastern Germans tried to save their country. But did they succeed in the end? At least their sacrifice stands out as proof that not all Germans were in agreement with Hitler's criminal policies, which brought so much chaos and suffering onto the world, and so much disgrace onto the Germans themselves:

Who succeeds?—Murky question.
Muffled Fate turns taciturn,
When, in times of utter gloom,
The bleeding nation's numb and mute.
Hear! New songs will yet redeem you,
Be no longer deeply bowed:
For the earth engenders music,
As it always has before.[7]

# 2

# The Expulsion Prehistory: Interbellum Years and World War II

The expulsion of entire populations at the end of armed conflicts was not in the European tradition. With the exception of the Greek-Turkish exchange of 1923 to 1926, European statesmen did not contemplate or carry out resettlement schemes prior to World War II. Of course, such schemes were not drawn up in a vacuum but were engendered by the so-called minorities problem, which had been exacerbated by the reordering of European states in 1919-20 as a consequence of World War I.

Before 1914 the European map was quite different. Most Germans lived in either the Bismarck Reich or in the Austro-Hungarian Empire. Ethnic Germans engaged primarily in agriculture could be found in czarist Russia and in the Balkans; in the Baltics, as businessmen and landowners, they belonged to the middle classes and the nobility. They lived in peace with their respective non-German neighbors. The more distinct problem of "German minorities" in Europe derives from the excesses of nationalism, which became especially acute after World War I, when new borders were imposed in 1919 by the peace treaties of Versailles, St. Germain and Trianon.

## THE PARIS PEACE CONFERENCE OF 1919

In his Fourteen Points speech of January 8, 1918, and in similar appeals to the warring parties, President Woodrow Wilson spoke out in favor of a fair and just peace and advocated national self-determination. In a noteworthy address delivered before both Houses of Congress on February 11, 1918, he emphasized that "peoples and provinces are not to be bartered about from sovereignty to sovereignty as if they were chattels and pawns in a great game, even the great game, now forever discredited, of the balance of power."[1] The Paris Peace Conference did not heed Wilson's admonition. The right to self-determination, to cultural identity, was not recognized for the vanquished. Millions of Germans were indeed bartered about from one state authority to another, for the balance-of-power principle was not abandoned.

Before World War I certain Slavic peoples had not yet attained self-determination, among them the Poles, Czechs, Slovaks, Croats, Slovenes and Serbs. In the name of their ideal, namely the foundation of a southern Slavic state, Serbian nationalists assassinated the Austrian crown successor and his wife in Sarajevo on June 28, 1914, thereby creating the *casus belli* of the Great War. During the war Slavic nationalists continued in their efforts to achieve full self-determination.

The Czechs were particularly successful in this regard, represented in the United States by the able intellectuals and diplomats Thomas Masaryk and Eduard Benes. First they won over Slovakian representatives in the United States to the concept of a common state wherein Slovakian autonomy was assured. They finally obtained the support of President Wilson who, in point 10 of his Fourteen Points, included autonomy for Slavs in the dual monarchy. Now, however, the intention was no longer to grant autonomy to the Slavs but to dissolve the multinational state of Austria-Hungary altogether.

In 1918-19 each Slavic successor state to the Danubian monarchy received not only its own ethnics, but also substantial numbers of national minorities as part of the overall population. Over five million ethnic Germans were left stranded outside of Austria, forming, as it were, a potential critical mass in Czechoslovakia, Hungary, Italy, Poland and Yugoslavia. The Treaty of St. Germain cut Austria off from its industries and resources, which were predominantly situated in the German-inhabited regions of Austrian Silesia and the Sudetenland. All that was left was a core state around a sharply reduced population of scarcely 7 million. The multinational Austria-Hungary had been cut to pieces. And yet, simultaneously, the multinational state of Czechoslovakia was established. In addition to Czechs (46%) and Slovaks (13%), it embraced a conglomerate of Poles (2%), Ruthenes (3%), Hungarians (8%) and 3.5 million Germans (28%).

Of course the German representatives, including the Social Democrats under Josef Seliger, similarly demanded the right to self-determination. However, their resolutions were not acknowledged at the Paris Peace Conference. It was only the American Expert Commission under the direction of Harvard Professor Archibald Coolidge that, during the peace negotiations, in a report to the American delegation dated March 10, 1919, pointed out that the Germans might possibly prove to be "indigestible." Coolidge summarized: "To grant to the Czechoslovaks all the territory they demand would be not only an injustice to millions of people unwilling to come under Czech rule, but it would also be dangerous and perhaps fatal to the future of the new state."[2]

The dangers foreseen by Coolidge moved him to suggest that the border in upper and lower Austria approach as nearly as possible the existing ethnic boundaries, while in the west the Eger district, not part of the original Bohemia, should be incorporated within Bavaria if it so desired. The German industrial regions of northern Bohemia should be allowed to become part of Saxony, with contested areas to be decided in favor of the Czechs. The Sudeten Mountains area, which could be "easily separable from Bohemia and Moravia," should be given the opportunity "to exist as a small state in the new German republic or be united to Prussian Silesia."[3] These suggestions would still have left a few hundred thousand Germans under Czech authority, an unavoidable situation as there were several areas where Germans and Czechs were fairly mixed. The recommendations made by the Coolidge Commission and the repeated protests of the Austrian government were completely ignored when the final borders were imposed. Contested regions were not given the benefit of a plebiscite; they were summarily awarded to Czechoslovakia.

An additional 1.5 million Germans remained as minorities in the other successor states to Austria-Hungary. Half a million who, depending on their province of residence, had formerly regarded Vienna or Budapest as their capital city found themselves inside the borders of the new Yugoslavian state: Swabians of the Banat, Batschka, Syrmia and Slovenia were the communities chiefly affected. Left in Romania were 750,000 Germans, mostly Siebenbuergen Saxons, Banat, Bessarabian and Bukovina Germans.

After the Treaty of Trianon, 550,000 Germans were consigned to what was left of Hungary. Unlike the Sudeten Germans, the Hungarian Germans were so widely dispersed among the native population that there could be little question of autonomy or self-determination. It would not have been feasible to draw any border in Hungary based on ethnic lines.

But in Italy, where such a border south of the Tyrol would have been possible, the victorious powers drew it farther north in order to redeem old political pledges. Italy had entered the war in 1915 on the side of the Entente based on guarantees contained in a secret treaty signed in London. South Tyrol was promised to Italy for its stand against the Central Powers, with a "strategic border" formed by the Brenner Pass. The Peace Treaty of St. Germain forced Austria to relinquish the territory in accordance with the secret arrangement, even though a mere 3% of the population (242,000 total) were of Italian extraction.

The Treaty of Versailles also denied the right of self-determination to Germans who had been citizens of the Reich but who resided in areas that were now separated from prewar German territory. Without a plebiscite, Danzig was declared a free city, while the province of Posen and the major portion of West Prussia were awarded to Poland.

Plebiscites were held, however, in Marienwerder and Allenstein, yielding majorities of over 90% in favor of remaining with Germany. A 1921 plebiscite in Upper Silesia resulted in a vote of 59.6% for Germany; due to Polish uprisings under Voiciech Korfanty, the League of Nations Commission decided not to award Upper Silesia to Germany but to partition it, and in such a way as to grant Poland the lion's share of land and natural resources. The Polish area included the cities of Kattowitz and Königshuette, which had voted 85% and 75% respectively for continued union with Germany.

Many Germans also lived in regions surrendered to Poland by Russia and Austria—central Poland, Lodz, Volhynia, Galicia and the Teschener Silesia. All in all, the new state of Poland was "home" to a German minority of more than 2 million souls.

Since the several Parisian treaties had left so many people of German descent outside the borders of Germany and Austria, there came an attempt to protect the principle of nationality by means of minority rights treaties framed under the aegis of the League of Nations. Poland and Czechoslovakia pledged to grant German minorities a certain measure of cultural autonomy, and further guaranteed legal parity with the Slavic majority.

In reality, both states found these obligations to be a burden in later years. They repeatedly declared that the system of minority rights protection constituted an intolerable infringement on their national sovereignty. Therefore the breach of the minorities treaties became the rule rather than the exception.

The German minorities were not everywhere subject to such treatment, however. There was less discrimination against them in the Baltic states than in Poland or Czechoslovakia. Between the wars 30,000 Germans lived in Lithuania, 70,000 in Latvia and 20,000 in Estonia. In Estonia and Latvia all German-owned farms were reduced to 50 hectares (125 acres) each. Any holdings exceeding that size were confiscated. The reduced acreage was economically inadequate with regard to then current levels of per-acre productivity. In Latvia the Germans were also oppressed in other ways. Still, life was better in Estonia, primarily as a result of Estonian legislation drafted in 1925 that introduced effective ways for exercising cultural self-determination by national minorities. Unfortunately, this example was not followed by either Poland or Czechoslovakia.

## GERMANS IN POLAND AND CZECHOSLOVAKIA, 1919 TO 1938

Between 1919 and 1934 several thousand protests were lodged with the League of Nations by Germans in Poland and Czechoslovakia pointing to violations of the Minority Rights Treaty of July 28, 1919.

The main causes for complaint were the extensive confiscations of German farms in Poland and the eviction of the German owners. One typical case came before the Permanent Court of Justice at The Hague, which, on September 10, 1923, rendered an opinion. The court found "that the measures complained of were a virtual annulment of legal rights possessed by the farmers under their contracts, and, being directed in fact against a minority and subjecting it to discriminating and injurious treatment to which other citizens holding contracts of sale or lease were not subject, were a breach of Poland's obligations under the Minorities Treaty."[4]

Similar cases were heard in courts or argued in petitions submitted to the League of Nations up until 1934, when the Polish government unilaterally withdrew from the League's minorities system.

Nobody would expect minorities who were so consistently discriminated against to entertain a positive attitude toward the host state. They fulfilled their civic duties, served in the Polish army, adhered to the laws and behaved as loyal citizens. But to demand beyond that a patriotic posture whereby one's loyalty was proved went against common sense and human nature. And yet this kind of patriotism was demanded of the Germans, people who were artificially made into a minority in a foreign state by virtue of the Treaty of Versailles of 1919. A vicious circle was thus created that finally brought down the entire structure of minority rights protection established by the League of Nations.

Hitler's ascension to power in Germany in 1933 did little, at first, to change the condition of the *Volksdeutsche* (the name given ethnic Germans outside the Reich and holding citizenship in their respective countries of residence). He concluded a nonaggression pact and a treaty of friendship with Poland on January 26, 1934; the *Volksdeutsche* were still not a component of Hitler's politics. Gradually he discovered their propaganda value and came to use their legitimate claims in an ill-willed agitation against the Poles and Czechs.

National Socialist infiltration of several cultural organizations caused some formerly dissatisfied *Volksdeutsche* gradually to become outright disloyal elements, people who would later play a role in Hitler's expansionist policies. Thus the leader of the Sudenten German Party, Konrad Henlein, turned to Hitler for help in obtaining Sudeten German self- determination. Henlein's demands outlined in the so-called Karlsbad Program of April 1938, for example, had already been orchestrated with Hitler. As expected, Czech President Benes rejected the program, giving Hitler the opportunity to escalate the international tension with open threats of force.

Czech government policies had unfortunately given cause to Henlein's activities. The unemployment rate among the Sudeten Germans was high, and they were discriminated against in not only civil service jobs but also in the private sector. Professor Arnold Toynbee, who had visited Czechoslovakia in 1937, wrote in *The Economist*:

> When you talk to a Czech about the minorities problem in Czechoslovakia, he is apt to begin by making the general statement that Czechoslovakia is a democracy. And when you talk to a member of the German minority, you find that this Czech claim to be democratic is like a red flag to a bull.
>
> The truth is that even the most genuine and old-established democratic way of life is exceedingly difficult to apply when you are dealing with a minority that does not want to live under your rule. We know very well that we ourselves were never able to apply our own British brand of democracy to our attempt to govern the Irish. And in Czechoslovakia to-day the methods by which the Czechs are keeping the upper hand over the Sudetendeutsch are not democratic.
>
> In their post-war intercourse with the Western peoples whom they so pathetically admire, the British infection which the Czechs have caught is not "effortless superiority," but "British hypocrisy," and they have taken it strong! Of all the burdens that the Czechs are carrying to-day, this vein of disingenuousness is perhaps the worst.[5]

As the situation deteriorated during the summer of 1938, Viscount Walter Runciman, confidant of British Prime Minister Neville Chamberlain, traveled to Prague and the Sudetenland on a peace-making mission. He spoke with both sides, and failed. In a report to Chamberlain he confirmed that:

> Czech officials and Czech police, speaking little or no German, were appointed in large numbers to purely German districts; Czech

agricultural colonists were encouraged to settle on land confiscated under Land Reform in the middle of the German populations; for the children of these Czech invaders Czech schools were built on a large scale; there is a very general belief that Czech firms were favored as against German firms in the allocation of State contracts, and that the State provided work and relief for Czechs more readily than for Germans. I believe these complaints to be in the main justified. Even as late as the time of my mission, I could find no readiness on the part of the Czechoslovak Government to remedy them on anything like an adequate scale. . . .

For many reasons, therefore, including the above, the feeling among the Sudeten Germans until about three or four years ago was one of hopelessness. But the rise of Nazi Germany gave them new hope. I regard their turning for help to their kinsmen and their eventual desire to join the Reich as a natural development in the circumstances.[6]

Not all Sudeten Germans looked for a radical solution. The large Sudeten German Social Democratic movement under Wenzel Jaksch and Ernst Paul wanted nothing to do with Hitler. They sought autonomy for the Sudeten Germans but no union with Nazi Germany. And following the Munich Agreement of 1938, they had to flee for their lives and become exiles in Great Britain or the United States.

Even in Germany certain circles rejected Hitler's machinations in the Sudeten question. Responsible officers did not want an European war and actually decided to arrest Hitler in order to put an end to his irresponsible and deadly game. General Ludwig Beck together with Generals Franz Halder, Hans Oster and Erwin von Witzleben drafted plans for a coup d'etat. But the "appeasement politics" of British Prime Minister Chamberlain frustrated these plans.

Chamberlain's personal mediation of the crisis was, to begin with, accomplished in the negotiations held at Berchtesgaden on September 15 and 16, 1938, wherein he recognized the Sudeten right of national self-determination. Based on the report submitted by Lord Runciman, on September 19, 1938, the British and French governments urgently advised the Czechs to cede the Sudetenland to the German Reich against a guarantee of new borders. On September 21 the Czechoslovak government accepted the Anglo-French proposal. In spite of this, the second meeting between Hitler and Chamberlain, held at Bad Godesberg from September 22 to 24, was a failure due to additional demands made by Hitler. The moment was now ripe for General Beck's coup. But Chamberlain made new concessions, and Hitler took full advantage of the unprecedented appeasement overtures.

This was followed by the intercession of Benito Mussolini, which culminated in the Munich Conference on September 29. French Prime Minister Edouard Daladier, Chamberlain, Mussolini and Hitler were present. The Czechs were not represented. The Munich Agreement regulated only the conditions and the modalities of the occupation of the Sudentenland by the Reich, not the Czech cession of the region, which in any case the Czech government had already stipulated to Britain and France on September 21. On the morning of September 30, 1938, the Czechoslovak foreign minister, Kamil Krofta, told the French, English and Italian ambassadors that his government would accept the decision reached in Munich.

For a moment, the world could breathe easy. "Peace in our time" was Chamberlain's sincere belief.[7] Though many regarded the agreement made with Hitler as repugnant, the alternative of war was worse. Subsequently Toynbee wrote of a "feeling of acute moral discomfort" at the prospect of "fighting for balance of power in defiance of the principle of nationality."[8]

In a supplementary declaration to the Munich Agreement, England and France reiterated their September 21 guarantee with regard to the new Czech-German border. Hitler declared his willingness to grant a similar guarantee after Czechoslovakia had also settled the question of Polish and Hungarian minorities. Europe took Hitler at his word, his assurance formulated in a speech held at the Sportpalast on September 26, 1938: "After this problem has been solved, there will be no further territorial problem for Germany in Europe."[9] But on March 15, 1939, barely half a year later, German troops marched into Prague. Bohemia and Moravia became a so-called Reich Protectorate alongside an autonomous state of Slovakia. Hitler's credibility abroad had been dubious before. With this play he lost it entirely. He had used the concept of self-determination solely as a means to an end. He now quickly repudiated it, since he thought it was of no further use to him.

Still, for the sake of historical perspective, the point must be made that Hitler *did* justify his move into Czechoslovakia. In a speech before the Reichstag on April 28, 1939, he cataloged the cultural and economic ties that had for many centuries evolved between Germany and Bohemia and Moravia. After all, Prague had been the capital of the Holy Roman Empire in the fourteenth century, and home to the oldest German-language university, founded there on April 7, 1346. Of more immediate importance to Hitler was the fact that the apparent politics of Anglo-French encirclement of Germany through guarantees or promises to Poland and Czechoslovakia had forced his hand. The London *News Chronicle* for July 14, 1938, quoted French Air Minister Pierre Cot, who said that in the case of any conflict with Germany, Czechoslovakia was to serve as "an aerodrome for the landing and taking-off of bombers, from which it would be possible to destroy the most important German industrial centres in a few hours."

Hitler was able to win territory without going to war on only one other occasion. On March 22, 1939, the "Memelland came home to the Reich." The "liberation" of the Hanseatic city of Danzig, placed under League of Nations protection by the Treaty of Versailles and granted a special status vis-à-vis Poland, was to follow, naturally pursuant to its right to self-determination. But the English and the French no longer accepted this argument.

The Nazi press raged: "*Volksdeutsche* Murdered in Poland," "German Mothers Terrorized," "Renewed Border Clashes." Hitler needed some justification in order to trigger a war against Poland. It was true that Germans in Poland had a hard time of it, that isolated outrages and murders did take place and that many Germans had been imprisoned. But Goebbels' propaganda exaggerated the situation. The Poles were aware of what had happened to the Czechs a few months earlier. They hesitated to negotiate over Danzig for they had seen through Hitler. They had no desire to become his next victim. This was not a question of Danzig or self-determination; it was a question of survival for the Polish state. As early as March 31, 1939, two weeks after the German occupation of Bohemia and Moravia, the Poles had secured a guarantee from England and France.

Hitler thought little of the guarantee. So he sought an ally in the East. For some time Joseph Stalin had been negotiating with the West. A treaty directed against Germany had been discussed but was wrecked through Stalin's territorial claims on the Baltic states, claims that London and Paris were not prepared to indulge. On the other hand, Hitler sacrificed the Baltics and found in Stalin an equally cold-blooded partner. A secret agreement was drawn up between Soviet Foreign Minister Vyacheslav Molotov and his German colleague Joachim von Ribbentrop. Poland was to be divided between the two signatory states. On September 1, 1939, Hitler grabbed Danzig and thereby unleashed the war.

## POLISH ATROCITIES AGAINST GERMANS
## FOLLOWING COMMENCEMENT OF HOSTILITIES

The first victims of the war were *Volksdeutsche,* ethnic German civilians resident in and citizens of Poland. Using lists prepared years earlier, in part by lower administrative offices, Poland immediately deported 15,000 Germans to Eastern Poland. Fear and rage at the quick German victories led to hysteria. German "spies" were seen everywhere, suspected of forming a fifth column. More than 5,000 German civilians were murdered in the first days of the war.[10] They were hostages and scapegoats at the same time. Gruesome scenes were played out in Bromberg on September 3, as well as in several other places throughout the province of Posen, in Pommerellen, wherever German minorities resided. German military magistrates were ordered to investigate atrocities committed against the German minority. Some 593 witnesses were interrogated under oath.[11] A few examples of these transcripts follow.

## The Testimony of Martha Kutzer

The testimony of Martha Kutzer was taken under oath before Judge Ulrich Schattenberg on September 10, 1939, in Bromberg.[12]

*On Sunday, September 3, 1939, soldiers again forced their way into our home to conduct a search for weapons. The men had to wait out in the yard. The soldiers demanded the motorcycle owned by my son, the Rev. Richard Kutzer. My son had to keep his arms raised while a soldier got on the motorcycle, asking how it worked. Eventually my son was taken away by the soldiers. They were just kids, 16 and 17 years old. Just as they got to the corner of the street I saw them hit my son in the stomach with a rifle butt. I saw this from a window. My son stumbled around a bit. Then one of the soldiers hit him again, this time across the shoulders. My son fell to the ground, writhing in pain. They stood him upright and ordered him to raise his hands again. Then they led him away. My husband, Otto Kutzer, and a man named Richard Hoffmann saw this, too. Both are now dead as well.*

## The Testimony of Lisbeth Busse

On October 14, 1939, Judge Hans Boetticher took the deposition of Fraulein Lisbeth Busse.[13]

*The Polish military killed both my parents, Franz and Ida Busse, my aunt Klara Busse, and my fiancé Erwin Dietrich.*

*During the night of Monday to Tuesday, September 4th and 5th, my father and fiance had fled into the woods. There was a lot of shooting going on. We all thought that the Germans were coming. A woman came by who said it was Polish soldiers who were everywhere, not Germans. She said we had to run for our lives, which is what I did. I fled in the company of our 20-year-old*

*farmhand Hans Neubauer. We likewise took off for the woods.*
*After only a couple of hours we were captured by Polish soldiers.*
*They took us to another soldier who must have been a senior*
*officer; he kept giving orders to those around him. I couldn't find*
*out what his rank was. I asked him if we could go back home. He*
*said, "What? You're Germans! We're going to blow you to pieces!"*
*Then I said, "Can I at least see my mother once more? She's still*
*back home." He said to another soldier, "Okay, take her back and*
*then shoot them both."*

*This other soldier then accompanied me and Neubauer back*
*home. But the place was empty. Apparently my mother and Aunt*
*Klara had fled. The soldier didn't know what to do. He said to*
*me, "If you do what I want, then you can stay here." When I*
*refused, he said we'll have to go to the command post. So off we*
*went. Along the way we met another group of soldiers. Our soldier*
*asked them where the command post was. When he was told that*
*it was quite a ways off, he said, "Then I'll shoot them here and*
*now. The commander is going to shoot 'em anyway, like all*
*German dogs." A few of the other soldiers said that it might not*
*be a good idea. While they talked over what they should do with*
*us, two or three more soldiers came along with a blindfolded man*
*in custody. When it turned out that they were taking him to the*
*command post, we were given over to these soldiers. Then we were*
*blindfolded too. We actually had to walk some of the way with*
*the blindfolds on. Finally we were told we had arrived. The*
*soldiers standing around us kept telling us that we would soon be*
*shot. Finally someone came over to us, a man who later turned*
*out to be the commander. He asked for the usual personal statistics*
*and eventually decided we were not to be shot. It was then that*
*the blindfolds were completely removed. We were given a certifi-*
*cate which stated we were Germans but with Polish citizenship.*
*We were given instructions to go to Hohensalza. When I said we'd*
*never get there, that soldiers along the way would shoot at us, he*
*sent a soldier to accompany us. He went as far as the main*
*highway with us. There were other people fleeing along the road,*
*and I went with them some 20 km beyond Kruschwitz. The Polish*
*paper I tore up.*

*I finally returned home on September 11, 1939. There I found*
*out that my father had been found shot dead at the edge of the*
*forest. On Thursday, September 14 I found the body of my fiancé*

*in a field not far from the Jesuitersee. September 14 was his birthday. He was lying there alone. He had a stab wound in his side, and he had been stabbed in his eyes. All his teeth had been knocked out.*

*My mother was found in the woods on September 17, 1939. She had been buried in a sitting position. She had three stabs in the intestinal region. My aunt Klara was found on 24 September 1939 on a field lying on her face. We recognized her from her clothes. I do not know what her injuries were.*

*I am all alone now. I have no brothers or sisters.*

## The Testimony of Adolf Duesterhoef

On September 20, 1939, Adolf Duesterhoef, a mason by trade, gave a deposition under oath before Judge Horst Reger.[14]

*On Monday, September 4, 1939, my son Arthur—born September 23, 1909—and I were arrested by the Polish military after we had been denounced by some Polish neighbors. We were taken to the police. We were accused of having been in radio contact with German pilots who had bombed Schwerenz the day before, and hit the garden of a private home. There had been no loss of life, however, even though the house near the garden had been occupied. Although I was not beaten on the way to the police station, my son was hit several times by civilians known to us. Toward evening I was released and could go back home. The next day my son and some other German prisoners were tied up, loaded onto a wagon and taken farther east.*

*On Sunday, September 10, 1939, a neighbor woman told me that she had heard my son and her husband had been shot by the Poles. The rumor turned out to be true, for on September 14, 1939, the bodies came back to Schwerenz and I had the chance to see the remains of my son and Mr. Kelm, a laborer. Both bodies had the same kinds of injuries: the bones in the face were completely smashed, the eyes had been gouged out, and the bodies bore several gunshot wounds. Additionally, my son's stomach had been cut open so that the intestines were falling out. I heard that the bodies of the other Germans were the same way.*

*My whole family had been Polish citizens and we had all done our civic duty vis-à-vis the Polish state. My son had served two years in the Polish army. My son and daughter were members of the Young German Party, but otherwise never politically involved against the Poles.*

## The Testimony of Dietrich Schmeichel

On October 14, 1939, Dietrich Schmeichel of Thorn reported before Judge Reger on the forced deportation marches.[15]

*On September 3, 1939, my two brothers and I were arrested by Polish soldiers being led by a lieutenant. We were taken to jail. The reason for our arrest was that we had supposedly given flashlight signals to German pilots. This was not true. On the way to the jail we were badly mistreated by the Polish mobs. My nose was broken. My brother received a serious neck wound. The guard soldiers just laughed at all this and even encouraged the mob by shouting, "Look everybody! German spies!"*

*Just before noon we began our march to internment that led from Thorn to Warsaw via Alexandrovo-Kutno. Our numbers consisted of men ranging in age from 16 to around 80 years old, about 50 women and one child aged 4. Because of detours our march was some 350 km, which had to be made on foot and without provisions or water. Even as we were just getting started we had to suffer the blows of rifle butts, being kicked, and stabbed with bayonets. . . . I myself got 10-15 stab wounds and rifle blows. The stab wounds were minor, but drew a lot of blood. I saw one comrade get stabbed in the buttocks by a Polish militia man. There was no reason for this mistreatment. After we had passed Alexandrovo a comrade tried to dash off to relieve himself behind a tree. He was immediately shot dead by a militia man. This caused a panic among us Germans. For fear of being similarly shot, they tried to flee and were immediately shot at. Thirty to 40 compatriots were thus shot to death or badly wounded by rifle fire. I personally saw these many bodies. One woman was severely wounded, lying on the ground and screaming in pain. This caused our transport commander, the notorious Captain Drzewiecke, or his adjutant, a corporal—I don't remember exactly which one— to shoot the woman six times with his Browning pistol in an attempt to finally kill her. But after the six additional shots she was still not dead. Because the woman continued to scream, the officer ordered one of the soldiers to kill her with a rifle shot. The soldier fired once at the woman and the screaming stopped. . . . According to my own observations and certain conviction, approximately 200 comrades lost their lives on that march, shot, stabbed or beaten to death. I heard a lot of gunfire along with horrible screams in the column behind me. Many of the comrades became disoriented, half crazy with the stress, deprivation and fear. Like the farmer Rohr, from Rittershausen near Lessen, and Laudetzke, a homeowner in Thorn who lived at No. 6 Warsaw Street, and a man known to me only as Stefan. All these comrades were killed.*

### The Testimony of Max Temme

The newly installed mayor of Schepanovo, Max Temme, gave the following deposition under oath before Judge Zornig on October 28, 1939.[16]

*I cannot speak from personal experience regarding the executions which took place in Schepanovo, as I was away from August 24 through October 2. I had been drafted into the Polish army, was then captured and imprisoned by the Germans on September 15, and finally released to return home on October 2, 1939.*

*The town of Schepanovo has around 950 inhabitants, 20% of them German.*

*On September 5 and 6 a total of 48 Germans were shot, 12 from Schepanovo itself, the rest from other communities.*

*The following people from my town were shot:*
*Hugo Rahn, age 51;*
*Erich Rahn, age 34;*
*Hilmar Lange, age 32;*
*Paul Lange, age 28;*
*Richard Klingbeil, age 46;*
*Adolf Wenzel, age 28;*
*Martin Prier, age 18;*
*Ewald Mueller, age 25;*
*Max Schuelke, age 32;*
*Wilhelm Patzer, age 60;*
*August Pansegrau, age 67;*
*Erich Pansegrau, age 29.*

> *The executions were carried out in groups, in both a forest quite close by and a field inside the town. Polish soldiers were responsible for the shootings, under orders of an officer. Among those shot were two women. I don't know their names since they came from different communities. The executions were completely unwarranted. None of these Volksdeutsche had taken any antagonistic position relative to the resident Poles here or the Polish military. And more to the point, none of these Germans had hidden away weapons, or taken shots at any Pole.*

The five testimonies quoted here are representative of hundreds more in a similar vein contained in the German Federal Archives and in the archives of other nations. To this day there are still witnesses to these events living in Germany and elsewhere, people who recall with terror and agony the events of September 1939 in Poland.

## HITLER'S "*LEBENSRAUM*" POLICIES

There can be no doubt that the *Volksdeutsche* suffered great injustice. But one must not forget the terrible revenge taken against the Polish people in the aftermath of the German victory. Thousands of Poles were executed arbitrarily. The Polish state was dissolved. Large Polish territories were annexed by the Reich; the rest as far as the Ribbentrop-Molotov line remained occupied and was administered by a regional government under the notorious Hans Frank, later convicted and hanged at Nuremberg. Approximately 1 million Poles were deported to this part of German-occupied Poland, an act of barbarism harshly condemned by the Polish government-in-exile in London.

On October 6, 1939, in a long speech before the Reichstag, Hitler was already referring to "a new order in ethnographic conditions, that is, a resettlement of the various nationalities which, upon completion, will yield lines of separation more clearly defined than is the case today."[17] This meant that Hitler intended to use the reservoir of several million *Volksdeutsche,* then inhabiting various countries in eastern and southeastern Europe, for his newly won "*Lebensraum.*" He signed a decree on October 7 by which all Germans threatened with "de-Germanization" were to be transferred to the Reich. On October 15 the Reich concluded an agreement with Estonia for the resettlement of 12,900 "splinters of German ethnicity"; this was followed on October 30 by an agreement with Latvia pertaining to an additional 48,600 Baltic Germans. Next, on November 3, an agreement was signed with the Soviet Union regarding 128,000 Germans from Volhynia and East Galicia. One year later there followed an agreement for the resettlement of 136,000 Bessarabian Germans, 66,000 Bukovina and Dobrudscha Germans and the rest of the Baltic Germans who in 1939 had opted for Latvia or Estonia, in the meantime occupied by the Soviet Union. It was time for them all to "come home to the Reich."

The resettlers were told their new homesteads would be situated on state-owned domains or lands otherwise not privately held. With these assurances the *Volksdeutsche* decided to leave their often centuries-old settlements. But the truth was something else: They were consigned to farms and homesteads whose Polish owners had just recently been evicted. This caused considerable moral shock for many resettlers. Several even refused to accept the homes and farms consigned to them. In spite of the situation, many newcomers quickly established good relations with their Polish workers, for they had been used to living with other ethnic groups. This was especially true of the Baltic landowners.

Following the German victory over France in 1940, the provinces of Alsace and Lorraine, which historically had been German before King Louis XIV annexed them to France in the late seventeenth century, and again from 1871 to 1918, following the German-Prussian war and until the end of World War I, were returned to the Reich. The "inconvenient" or "recalcitrant" French population of the region, around 100,000 people, was deported to Vichy France. In 1941 it was Yugoslavia's turn, and once again the German occupation authorities evicted thousands from home and hearth.

Reacting to these measures, representatives of the occupied nations exiled in London declared as early as January 13, 1942: "With respect to the fact that Germany, from the beginning of the present conflict, has erected regimes of terror in the occupied territories . . . characterized in particular by . . . mass expulsions . . . , the undersigned representatives . . . set among their primary war aims the punishment of those responsible for these crimes in accordance with accepted rules of law."[18] In London the Polish cabinet-in-exile issued a decree on October 17, 1942, that sanctioned the death penalty for deportations and forced resettlement.[19]

Besides the expulsions for the *Lebensraum* policies, millions of non-Germans were deported to the Reich and made to work in the war industries. They were often treated as subhumans who were meant to work for the "master race." Their accommodations were inhuman and degrading. And then there were the concentration camps. Many thousands would not survive long enough to be liberated by the Allies; and many died shortly after their liberation owing to disease or malnourishment. The practice of genocide in the camps became the ultimate crime.

## HITLER'S POLICIES OF EXPULSION
## AT THE NUREMBERG TRIALS

The catalog of crimes committed by the National Socialist government of Germany was so large that an international court was convened in Nuremberg in 1945 to bring those responsible to trial.

Reich Marshal Hermann Goering, Foreign Minister Joachim von Ribbentrop, Field Marshal Wilhelm Keitel and Reich Labor leader Fritz Sauckel and Alfred Rosenberg were accused of, among other crimes, forced expulsion of civilian populations, mass deportations for the purposes of gaining *Lebensraum* and forced labor.

Article 6(b) of the court statutes defined war crimes as follows: "murder, ill treatment or *deportation* to slave labor or *for any other purpose* of civilian population of or in occupied territory. . . ."[20] Article 6(c) defined "crimes against humanity"[21] as follows: "murder, extermination, enslavement, *deportation* and other inhumane acts committed against any civilian population *before* or during the war."

Count 3, Section B, of the Nuremberg indictment concerned the "[d]eportation for slave labor and for other purposes of civilian populations of and in occupied territories."

Count 3, Section J, of the indictment read:

> In certain occupied territories purportedly annexed to Germany the defendants methodically and pursuant to plan endeavored to assimilate these territories politically, culturally, socially, and economically into the German Reich. They endeavored to obliterate the former national character of these territories. In pursuance of their plans, the defendants *forcibly deported* inhabitants who were predominantly non-German and replaced them by thousands of German colonists."[22]

Count 4, Section A, dealt with crimes against humanity, including the crime of mass deportation.

During the trials, the practice of "Germanizing" occupied or "annexed" territories was repeatedly condemned, as were the deportations of civilian populations from one occupied region to another occupied region (the Government General of Poland), or to nonoccupied regions (Vichy France) or to serve as forced labor in the Reich.[23] Pierre Mounier, assistant prosecutor for the French Republic, reproached the accused on November 20, 1945, the first day of the trials, for having ordered the mass deportations: "These deportations were contrary to the international conventions, in particular to Article 46 of the Hague Regulations, 1907, the laws and customs of war, the general principles of criminal law as derived from the criminal laws of all civilized nations, the internal penal laws of the countries in which such crimes were committed, and to Article 6(b) of the Charter."[24]

On January 17, 1946, Francois de Menthon, chief prosecutor for the French Republic, denounced these crimes: "Persons who appeared recalcitrant to Nazification, or even those who seemed of little use to Nazi enterprises, became victims of large-scale expulsions, driven from their homes in a few short hours with their most scanty baggage, and despoiled of their property. . . . [T]his inhumane evacuation of entire populations . . . will remain one of the horrors of our century."[25]

On February 1, 1946, Edgar Faure, deputy chief prosecutor for the French Republic, declared that the deportations and Germanization in France, Belgium and Luxembourg were "a criminal undertaking against humanity."[26] With respect to the expulsions in Poland, the assistant prosecutor for the United States remarked: "Poland was, in a sense, the testing ground for the conspirators' theories upon 'Lebensraum. . . .'[27] They planned to deport to the Government General many hundreds of thousands of Jews, members of the Polish intelligentsia and other non-compliant elements."[28]

On February 26, 1946, L. N. Smirnov, assistant prosecutor for the Soviet Union, again dealt with the matter of expulsions and read an official report into the court record:

> Locality after locality, village after village, hamlets and cities in the incorporated territories were cleared of the Polish inhabitants. This began in October, 1939 when the locality of Orlov was cleared of all the Poles who lived and worked there. Then came the Polish port of Gdynia. In February 1940, about 40,000 people were expelled from the city of Posnan. They were replaced by 36,000 Baltic Germans, families of soldiers and of German officials. The Polish population was expelled from the following towns: Gnesen, Kulm, Kostian, Neshkva, Inovrotzlav . . . and many other towns.[29]

Smirnov went on to say that "a similar Hitlerite crime was to have been committed in Yugoslavia. This crime could not be perpetrated because of the liberation movement which had flared up all over Yugoslavia. . . . The German plan foresaw the complete removal of all the Slovenes from certain regions of Slovenia, and their repopulation by Germans—Germans from Bessarabia and so-called 'Gottscheer' Germans."[30]

Citing from a German report on a conference held on June 4, 1941, at the German Legation in Zagreb under the title "The Expulsion of the Slovenes from Germany to Croatia and Serbia, as well as of Serbs from Croatia to Serbia," he noted: "The conference was approved by the Reich Ministry for Foreign Affairs by Telegram Number 389, dated 31 May. The Fuehrer's approval for the deportation was received by Telegram Number 344 dated 25 May."[31]

Counselor Smirnov concluded: "We are thus able to prove that the direct responsibility for this *crime against humanity* rests on the Defendant von Ribbentrop."[32]

The defense tried unsuccessfully to justify these crimes by denying the applicability of the Hague Convention and by referring to the principle of the *ultima ratio regum* (the last resort of the king) along with the new concept of "total war." On July 10, 1946, the court rejected the argument of Dr. Alfred Thoma, defense counsel for Alfred Rosenberg, that in a situation of total war, the deportation of civilians to another country for the purpose of forced labor, or for other purposes, as a method applied *in extremis* is permissible to avert one's own subjugation. The court was of the opinion that even in a total war, when a country must fight for its very existence, civil rights and in particular the Hague Convention and its Regulations on Land Warfare place nonderogable restraints upon those waging war.[33]

Similarly, on July 26, 1946, the main British prosecutor, Sir Hartley Shawcross, rejected the theory that "the prohibition of the Law of Nations relating to deportation had in some way become obsolete in the face of the modern development of totalitarian war."[34]

Consequently, the Nuremberg judgment held that mass deportations constituted both a war crime and a crime against humanity.

The anomaly remains that while the Nuremberg trials were in progress, millions of Germans were being driven from their homelands, based on decrees, or at least under the sanction, of the same powers whose prosecutors and judges were condemning the mass deportations perpetrated by the Nazis.

# 3

# War and Flight

Many today ignore or minimize the horrors of the expulsion of the Germans. Journalists and politicians seldom speak about it. When they do, they mention a "transfer of populations," which sounds harmless enough. Even historians in the East and in the West have had a tendency to use similar euphemisms. Yet, in order to understand how the Germans themselves perceive the expulsion, it is necessary to look for a more encompassing definition of the term *Vertreibung,* or expulsion, which is seen in Germany as embracing not only the mass expulsions in the summer and fall of 1945 but also the evacuations of German populations undertaken by German authorities beginning in the fall of 1944, the general flight of refugees in the spring of 1945 and the organized forced resettlements that began in 1946. The term is perceived in this manner because the evacuees and those who fled fully intended to return to their home regions at the conclusion of hostilities. However, Polish and Soviet authorities prevented the refugees from returning, thereby uprooting them and, in a very real sense, making expellees out of them.

This part of the book focuses on the dramatic move of millions of persons West, whether as refugees or expellees. Perhaps in order to better grasp the mercilessness and vehemence of this encounter of forces, it is useful to see it as the final chapter of the war of annihilation unleased by Hitler and known under the code name of Operation Barbarossa.

The German-Soviet war began on June 22, 1941, and from the start, it was waged differently from the war in Western Europe. Neither the German nor the Soviet side observed the rules of war, in particular, the conventions adopted at The Hague and Geneva. Special squads of German Security Service (SS) troops murdered hundreds of thousands of Soviet citizens, primarily Jews. Awful reprisals were exacted for every action of Soviet partisans. And, as is so often the case, most of the victims were innocent people.

The intentions of the so-called General Plan-East[1] were the forced deportations of 30 million Slavs to Siberia, to be followed by German settlement areas and outposts established in the vacated territories known as the four Reich Commissariats: Ostland, the Ukraine, Moskovia and the Caucasus.

A terrible revenge was inevitable should the course of the war turn against Germany. Would retaliation recognize limits? Would it even try to separate the guilty from the innocent? For centuries the human need to seek retribution for perceived injustice has been held in check by both moral principle and by law. But do these principles carry through to times of war? *Inter arma silent leges* (The law is silent in war). Is there then only the law of retribution, the *lex talionis?*

Operation Barbarossa was "total war"; it was savage on both sides. The passions of soldiers, rather than being held in check, were whipped into a frenzy.

An example on the Soviet side is the work of the "Soviet Julius Streicher," Ilya Ehrenburg, whose hate-mongering pamphlets and fliers were distributed at home and at the front:

> The Germans are not human beings. From now on the word "German" is for us the worst imaginable curse. From now on the word "German" strikes us to the quick. We shall not get excited. We shall kill. If you have not killed at least one German a day, you have wasted that day . . . If you cannot kill your German with a bullet, kill him with your bayonet. If there is calm on your part of the front, or if you are waiting for the fighting, kill a German in the meantime . . . If you kill one German, kill another—for us there is nothing more joyful than a heap of German corpses.[2]

In the military newspaper *Krasnaja Swesda* (Red Star) Ehrenburg wrote on October 24, 1944, just as the Red Army had crossed the Lithuanian-German border into East Prussia: "We are now in the homeland of Erich Koch, the governor of the Ukraine—that says it all. We have said it often enough: The day of judgment is coming! That day has arrived."[3] And: "It is not enough to drive the Germans west. The Germans must be driven into the grave. It is certainly better to have a dead Fritz than an impudent one. The best Fritz is a dead one."[4]

Ehrenburg did not hesitate to use the obscene Nazi language, which referred to other human beings as scorpions, plague-carrying rats, rabid dogs, microbes or bacteria. In many of his articles he vituperated as follows: "We are continuing Pasteur's work, who discovered the serum against rabies. We are continuing the work of all scientists who have discovered methods to destroy deadly microbes."[5]

Ehrenburg was by no means the only agitator. The writings of Alexei Tolstoy, K. M. Simonov, and A. A. Surkov, among many other hate-mongers, had their effect on the morale of the troops. A Soviet war correspondent, watching the city of Insterburg burning on January 25, 1945, wrote: "There is no more educational a spectacle than the sight of an enemy city in flames. One searches the soul for some sort of feeling akin to sympathy, but it cannot be found. . . . Burn, Germany, you have earned nothing better. I will not and shall not forgive what you have done to us. . . . Burn, accursed Germany."[6]

Stalin sought to quell world reaction to such words by issuing an order to his soldiers, Order of the Day No. 55, which read: "Occasionally there is talk that the goal of the Red Army is to annihilate the German people. . . . It would be foolish to equate the German people and the German State with the Hitler clique. The lessons of history tell us that Hitlers come and go, but the German people, the German State, they shall remain."[7]

Reasonable words, if Stalin could be taken seriously. The truth is, his fine words were not intended for his troops. They were uttered solely for their propaganda effect with the Western Allies.

Reality was quite a different matter for the civilian populations of East Prussia, Pomerania and Silesia—that is, for those who did not flee in time. And not only for the locals, but also for thousands upon thousands of refugees evacuated from their bombed-out cities and now fleeing the advancing Red Army, caught in the wrong place at the wrong time. Their numbers consisted primarily of women, the elderly and children.

## OCTOBER 1944 IN EAST PRUSSIA: NEMMERSDORF

On October 19, 1944, the first Soviet troops crossed the German frontier. The counties of Goldap and Gumbinnen were captured. Before the onslaught, most of the population of these counties, predominantly farmers, tried to flee. Many succeeded, but the inhabitants of the village Nemmersdorf in Gumbinnen began their evacuation too late. A German counteroffensive retook the region one week later.

## The Testimony of Dr. Heinrich Amberger

An eyewitness to the Soviet invasion of East Prussia, Dr. Heinrich Amberger, made the following report:

> *Scores of bodies lay in the gutters and in the yards of private homes, civilians all, who had obviously not been caught in any hostile crossfire, but rather intentionally murdered. I saw among them women who, by the state and position of their clothing, had certainly been raped, then killed by a shot through the base of the skull. In some cases their similarly murdered children lay next to them.*[8]

Swiss newspaper correspondents also reported on the events in Nemmersdorf. For instance, on November 7, 1944, the Geneva *Courier* published the eyewitness account of its special correspondent on the Eastern Front:

> *The war in East Prussia, currently unfolding in the triangle Gumbinnen-Goldap-Ebenrode, is at the centre of events, especially following the recapture of Goldap by the Germans. The situation cannot be described simply in terms of a bitter struggle between regular troops, or with reference to the enormous amount of weaponry used on both sides, or the last minute recruitment of a German civilian militia, but rather and unfortunately by all too well known methods of warfare: mutilations and executions of prisoners of war and the almost total annihilation of the German farming population, to the extent that these had remained in their lands in the late afternoon of October 20. . . . The German civilian population has virtually disappeared from the combat area, most peasants and their families having fled. With the exception of a young German woman and a Polish hand everyone has been killed by the Red Army. Thirty men, 20 women, 15 children fell in the hands of the Red Army at Nemmersdorf and were murdered. At Brauersdorf I myself saw two French farm hands, former prisoners of war, who had similarly been massacred. One of them could be identified. Not far away 30 German prisoners had suffered the same fate. I will spare you the description of the mutilations and the ghastly*

*condition of the corpses on the field. These are impressions that go beyond even the wildest imagination.*[9]

## The Testimony Of Emil Radüns

Emil Radüns, a member of the *Volkssturm,* or civilian militia, gave the following account:

> *On October 23, 1944, just before 8 A.M., I arrived in Nemmersdorf in the company of Regional Commissar Wurach. We had orders to ascertain whether or not people had been shot there. Entering the village from the west, we immediately saw nine bodies lying in a ravine. There were three women, three men and three children, all with head wounds. In the village itself we found a civilian shot dead in front of the fire station; another dead in the cow stall of his barn; a woman sitting in a room with her hands folded, shot dead. Her legs were covered by a comforter, which leads one to believe she didn't even resist or run off when her home was invaded. Her home had obviously been ransacked, everything was a mess. Another woman who had been shot was still crouching next to a wagon parked in the street; she had her hands in front of her face. Near the bridge, in front of a house, an elderly woman lay in the street next to a younger woman and a child. In one house I discovered a young woman whose legs were still spread apart. I remember her now as the same woman whom the doctor had examined, determining that she had been sexually assaulted. In that same room were the bodies of an old man and woman, both with head wounds. We put the bodies in order and carried them to the cemetery.*[10]

## The Testimony Of Hans Zirm

Atrocities were also reported from Alt-Wusterwitz, south of Gumbinnen. Lieutenant Hans Zirm reports:

> *On October 24, 1944, I moved with my Air Defense unit to the region west of Girnen, about 9 km south of Gumbinnen. In my search for lodging I came upon the farm town of Alt-Wusterwitz, where I made the following sad discovery:*
> *At one farm the Russians had gathered then murdered in a most bestial way every last civilian who had been unable to escape.*

*Six burned skeletons lay in the stalls, and next to them an almost completely naked young girl. She had been raped several times (her genitals were bloody) and then shot twice, in the chest and in the stomach. Another dead girl lay in the barn, similarly raped before being shot to death.[11]*

## FEBRUARY 1945 IN EAST PRUSSIA: METGETHEN

The fate of Nemmersdorf in October 1944 was repeated in untold numbers of East Prussian, Pomeranian and Silesian villages during the last months of the war. A particularly well documented massacre occurred in Metgethen, a suburb of Königsberg. It was occupied by the Soviet Army from January 29 to February 19, 1945, then recaptured by the German 5th Panzer and 1st Infantry Divisions. The outrages committed by Soviet soldiers, just three weeks in Metgethen, are described in a series of depositions preserved in the German Federal Archives.

B.H., a soldier, declared:

*During the course of the German offensive to reestablish the land link between Königsberg and Pillau from 19 to 24 February, 1945, we, the German soldiers of the attacking units, discovered the following crimes:*

*1. In the town of Metgethen, a western suburb of Königsberg, we found that many homes contained the bodies of women and children, ranging in age from 10 to 80, raped and murdered. We gathered about 200 of these bodies in troop carriers in an effort to identify them. . . .*

*2. At the Metgethen railway station we came upon approximately seven passenger coaches, part of a refugee train from Königsberg. In each car we found seven to nine bestially mutilated bodies of all ages and both sexes; certain women bearing the marks of rape.*

*3. A bomb crater about 10 meters across and 4 meters deep was found in the Metgethen tennis courts. Inside the crater and along its perimeter, in the area immediately surrounding it, on the high chain link fence around the courts and in the branches of nearby tall trees, lay and hung mud-covered bodies and body parts, about 25 men, women and children, three or four antiair-*

craft men, and a few men in German police uniforms. The cadavers of several horses also lay around the crater perimeter, among the remains of several wagons and their mangled loads of refugee belongings. We found still more parts of bodies, like a knee, a hand and arm, etc., up to 200 meters away from the crater. The explanation is obvious. The refugees, captured soldiers and policemen were driven into this existing bomb crater, the refugee wagons placed around it, and an explosive charge placed then detonated at the bottom of the crater in the midst of the trapped prisoners.[12]

Horst A., at the time a driver for the Intelligence Reserve Detachment I, Königsberg, reported:

When we reached Metgethen, we were confronted with a gruesome sight: We found several hundred dead German soldiers, many of whom had been disfigured beyond recognition. There were murdered civilians in just about every home, likewise disfigured in a most bestial manner. For example, some women had their breasts cut off, and in backyard gardens we found scarcely clad women who had been hanged upside down. In one house we came across a 63-year-old woman still alive. Crying, she told us that she had been raped by 12 to 15 Russians. She lay on the floor covered in blood. This old woman's daughter had escaped into the forest nearby, but her one-year-old child was abducted by the Russians. In the streets of Metgethen, and also at the railroad station, we found approximately 15 baby carriages, some overturned, all empty. We concluded that this meant the Russians had also abducted these babies.[13]

## The Testimony of Karl August Knorr

The deposition of Karl August Knorr is similar.

I was at the time an orderly officer in the 561st Civil Grenadier Division charged with the task of restoring order in Metgethen after it had been recaptured by our side. In one street I discovered the bodies of two young women, both about 20, who had apparently been tied by the legs, one limb each between two cars, and then torn apart when the vehicles were driven in opposite directions. It was *an absolutely disgusting sight. In that same street I came upon a large villa. I can't remember the name of the street. The house contained around 60 women, all of whom we evacuated from the area. Half of them had to be taken immediately to a psychiatric hospital . . . on average they had been raped 60 to 70 times a day.*[14]

## The Testimony of Hermann Sommer

A more elaborate report was made by a former captain in the Fortress Königsberg command staff, Hermann Sommer.

*A number of troop companies reported to the fortress commander the discovery of several mounds of corpses situated quite close to one another. The commander, General Lasch, ordered a commission to investigate these discoveries. The commission reported that many similar piles of bodies were strewn throughout the area; but in two cases there were virtual mountains of bodies made up of ca. 3,000 women, girls, children and only a few men. A special commission of doctors, forensic investigators and foreign journalists was formed to establish identities and the circumstances of the deaths. The work was made difficult by the fact that the Russians had poured gasoline on the mounds of bodies and attempted to burn them. Nevertheless many of the dead were photographed. The pictures graphically showed the often savage circumstances under which these people had been murdered. On the basis of these pictures and of the reports made by the forensics team, the conclusion was drawn that the victims had been beaten and stabbed; in very few cases were persons killed by a shot to the base of the skull. A large number of bodies had the breasts cut off, the genitals stabbed through and were disemboweled. The testimonies of witnesses, who had survived the raping and other physical abuse by the Russians, along with the photographs, are on file in my department. They were used by the security officers and officials of the criminal police to interrogate prisoners of war brought back from the Eastern Front; and to question civilians in the attempt to establish the identities of the victims. . . .*

*I made my own observations when I was sent to Metgethen on official business on February 27, 1945. Just on the outskirts of town near the first railway crossing, I turned my motorcycle into a gravel driveway so that I could look over a building and see if it was suitable for service use. Behind the building I suddenly came upon the bodies of 12 women and six children. Most of the children had been killed by a blow to the head with a blunt instrument, some had numerous bayonet wounds in their tiny bodies. The women, mostly between 40 and 60 years of age, had been killed with knife or bayonet. All of them bore the unmistakable black-and-blue marks of beatings.*

*After the first Soviet blockade had been completely smashed, I was ordered on February 28, 1945, to report to a unit of the 4th Army. On my way, I stopped for a rest in the village of Gross Heydekrug. I had arrived just as medics and civilians were burying some 35 mostly female bodies. Here again I saw the gruesome mistreatment practiced by the Russians, all shown to me by indignant soldiers and civilians. Most of the victims were again women. A corporal told me of a church where a girl and two soldiers had been found. The girl had been actually crucified on the altar cross, the two soldiers strung up on either side.*

*Farther into the village I saw civilian bodies lying everywhere, as far as the highway crossing to Powayen. While most of the men had been shot in the base of the skull, the women were completely naked, raped and then killed in the most brutal way with stab wounds or rifle butt blows to the head. At the highway crossing to Powayen stood a Soviet tank which had been dragging the now-dead bodies of four naked women behind it. A commission was already there taking photographs of the scene.*[15]

## The Testimony of Professor Dr. G. Ipsen

This account by Professor G. Ipsen is on file in the German Federal Archives.

*The mounds of bodies were without exception Germans, most of them not residents of Metgethen, but refugees who had been caught unawares by the Russian advance three weeks ago, and thus unable to flee farther west. The empty refugee trains still stood in the train station. . . . The incident of the crucifixion in Heydekrug is true. . . .*

*The survivors of Metgethen were mentally in a state that bordered on insanity. It was not possible to release them back into the city or to friends and relatives. Instead they were lodged in the spacious Park Hotel where, for more than a week, they*

*received medical treatment and were placed in the care of sisters.
They could only be released to private care after they had regained
some measure of emotional equilibrium, so that they no longer
posed a threat to themselves and their gruesome accounts would
not unduly alarm those who might come into contact with them.*[16]

For reasons best explained by a psychologist, one of the aberrations practiced by the soldiers was to take victims, mostly female, strip them naked and nail them to barn doors in cruciform fashion. This one particular atrocity features prominently in many eyewitness reports.

Every gruesome detail of the terrifying events in Metgethen was recorded on handbills distributed to the German civilian population, in order to spur a desperate resistance. At this point the Nazi leadership in Berlin, fearing the rapid advance of the Soviet Army, appealed to the historical sense of the beleaguered East Prussians. Goebbels had the propaganda film *Kolberg* flown to Königsberg and played everywhere. In this film director Veit Harlan tells the story of the Pomeranian citizens of Kolberg, who during the Franco-Prussian War of 1806-7, under the leadership of Generals Gneisenau and Nettelbeck, had prevented the surrender of their city to Napoleon's troops after the defeated Prussian army had fled into East Prussia. One hundred forty years later the Germans were urged to follow the example set by the citizens of Kolberg, to fight to the last man, never to capitulate.

## The Testimony of Hans Graf von Lehndorff

Hans Graf von Lehndorff, a medical doctor in Königsberg at the time it was occupied by the Soviet Army, writes in his diary under April 12, 1945:

*When it was dark our escort came with bulls-eye lanterns and
routed us all up. The women, whimpering or cursing, were
dragged out with the help of the Poles. This unending devilry!
"Davai suda!" "Woman come!" It has a more horrific sound than
all the curses in the world. When that which should signify Life
stands under the sign of Death, Satan's triumph has reached its
zenith. It didn't matter to them in the least that they were
handling semi-corpses. Eighty-year-old women were no safer from
them than the unconscious ones. (At one time a patient of mine
with head injuries, as I discovered later, had been raped over and
over again without knowing anything about it.)*[17]

## OFFICIAL WEHRMACHT INVESTIGATIONS

These and other excesses committed by the Soviet army were systematically investigated and recorded by the German Armed Forces legal department, as long as there was opportunity to interrogate witnesses. Besides the Armed Forces Investigations Bureau, the army intelligence department, known as the "Ic Department," in particular the Ic of "Foreign Armies-East," also conducted its own investigations. One Ic report, reads as follows:

Memorandum on the Behavior of the Red Army on German Territory, 22 February 1945:

> *The incursion of the Red Army into Reich territory was preceded by a systematic agitation on the part of military political divisions. The troops were told in their Front newspapers, at political assemblies and lectures, that they were given a free hand relative to the German population. Depositions taken from captured troops make repeated reference to a related order from Stalin, the original of which, however, is not in hand.*
>
> *The wording of previously captured calls "for revenge on behalf of our brothers and sisters, wives and children, mothers and fathers in Russia murdered by the fascists'" leaves no doubt in the minds of Red Army troops, that reprisals against German civilians, pillage, rape and so on are permissible. During political instruction they are further given more comprehensive, detailed oral directives, that is, even harsher interpretations of the published calls to vengeance.*
>
> *The result of this systematic agitation appears to have caused atrocities of such magnitude on the part of certain divisions and units that discipline is endangered by troops getting out of hand. For this reason Soviet leadership has obviously been compelled to put a stop to the worst infringements. Just how far orders issued in this regard have been put into practice cannot be measured as yet. The interrogations of prisoners of war, captured enemy reports and intelligence show that the average soldier in the Red Army, despite threatened draconian punishment, has nonetheless found ways to sabotage orders of restraint. . . .*
>
> *The experiences outlined below summarize the above-mentioned enemy reports and intelligence, as well as the anti-looting orders, and are offered here as established fact:*

*Looting*
The troops in the advance columns are often not in a position to carry out any looting, due to lack of time and sheer exhaustion. Whenever plunder is taken, it is mostly food, clothing, boots and jewelry that are stolen. The supply and rear-guard detachments that follow systematically loot every house, under the eyes of tolerant officers. Finished cloth of all types is the preferred booty (theft of furniture coverings, drapes, etc.). Moreover, as verified in prisoner interrogation, fully senseless destruction of household furnishings have been observed, such as destruction of furniture, clothing cut to shreds, dishes smashed and pictures torn up.

Although a general order was issued forbidding pillage, it was nevertheless followed by a systematic "requisitions action" initiated by the commissariats. Additionally, a recent authorization that permits Soviet soldiers to ship packages of 5 to 15 kg back home only encouraged the infractions.

While some troops are forbidden to engage in looting, the removal of evidence of pillage is often removed by simply putting the buildings to the torch.

*Rape*
The captured enemy orders ban specific violations of conduct, but rape is not mentioned. Reports from eyewitnesses and other sources attest to extensive occurrence of rape, usually under the influence of alcohol. Girls and women of all ages from 8 to 68 years old are violated, sometimes by up to 24 officers and Red Army regulars at a time, most often at gunpoint. In many cases, a gang rape is followed by murder. Captured enemy diaries and letters confirm these bestial events in detail.

*Executions and Other Reprisals*
Taken from the content of their own captured service reports and looting prohibitions, it is clear that the advancing enemy troops fire indiscriminately at the civilian population. Whenever Soviet tanks overtake columns of refugees on the roadways, the civilians are often shot en masse or rolled over and crushed beneath the tanks. There are, however, some isolated reports that indicate proper behavior in this regard. In these cases civilians are ordered to return to their homes and stay there.

*Troop behavior is essentially dependent on the disposition of the respective commanders. Reports intercepted up to this time indicate that most officers silently tolerate the atrocities, indeed, they often take part. Troop and field intelligence, for example in the area of the Fourth Army, tell of civilians being purposely driven from their homes during Soviet attacks to serve as live practice targets. . . .*[18]

*Although the Order of the Day issued at the start of the January 1945 offensive by the Supreme Commander of the 1st White Russian Front, Marshal Zhukov, made no direct call for looting or rape, its prevailing tone of retribution led troops to conclude as much. The text of the captured order runs as follows:*

> "To the soldiers, noncommissioned officers, officers and Generals; Troops of the 1st White Russian Front.
>
> Comrades-in-Battle!
>
> The great hour has tolled! The time has come to deal the enemy a last and decisive blow, and to thus fulfill the historical task set before us by Comrade Stalin: To finish off the fascist animal in his own lair and raise the banner of victory over Berlin!
>
> The time has come to reckon with the German fascist scoundrels. Great and burning is our hatred! We have not forgotten the pain and suffering done to our people by the Hitlerist cannibals. We have not forgotten our burned-out cities and villages. We remember our brothers and sisters, our mothers and fathers, our wives and children tortured to death by the Germans. We shall avenge those burned in the devil's ovens, avenge those who suffocated in the gas chambers, avenge the murdered and the martyred. We shall exact a brutal revenge for everything.
>
> We go to Germany. Behind us lies Stalingrad, the Ukraine and White Russia; we travel through the ashes of our cities and villages, treading on the blood stains left by our Soviet people tortured and hacked to death by the fascist beast.
>
> Woe to the land of the murderers! Nothing can stop us now!
>
> We have sworn to our fallen friends, to our children, that we shall not lay down our weapons until the evil-doers have been disposed of. The fascist bandits shall pay for the death and blood

*in our Soviet nation with every last drop of their own black and lowly blood.*

*The time has come, Comrades, to liberate the millions of our Soviet people dragged off and pressed into German slave labor. Their lives are in grave danger. The sooner we are in Germany, the more we can save. At the same time we shall help our brothers, the Poles, Czechs and other oppressed peoples in Europe, to throw off the chains of German slavery. By destroying the fascist beast we are fulfilling to the last degree our role as an army of liberation.*

*The war cannot end so long as Soviet people still languish in German slavery, so long as the fascist bandits' den has not been utterly smashed.*

*Comrades!*

*We face and must overcome a desperate enemy resistance. Caught in a vise of the two Fronts, between us and our allies, the enemy will wage an embittered opposition knowing they have been condemned to death. But beating the Germans is nothing new for us. Our Front troops have beaten them at Stalingrad and Kursk, on the Dnieper and in White Russia, on the Vistula and the Narev. We beat them even when they had the support of their allies, the Hungarians and Finns, the Romanians and Bulgarians. Their cohorts learned a hard lesson from us, the Red Army, and consequently turned their weapons against the Germans. The German is now alone, like a trapped animal. We beat the Germans when we were alone, and now together with the Americans and English, the French and Belgians we are beating them again.*

*This time we will destroy the German brood once and for all! . . .*"[19]

When even Marshal Zhukov incited his troops in this manner and did not attempt to call for respect of the lives of noncombatants, it is really no wonder that the Red Army massacred hundreds of thousands of German civilians. The unpleasant realities of war are revealed in the following excerpts taken from captured Red Army Field Postal Service letters:

"And now we take our revenge on the Germans for all their despicable acts committed against us. We're being allowed to do what we please with the German scoundrels."

"German mothers shall rue the day they gave birth to a son. May German mothers now feel the horrors of war firsthand. What they wanted to do to other people they will now experience themselves!"

"We spend the night in their houses and drive the Germans out into the cold, just like they did to us."

"There are only old people and children in Germany, very few girls. But we kill them all anyway."

"Now we're meeting up with German civilians, and our soldiers are making good use of German women."

"There are plenty of women around, but they don't understand a word of Russian. But that's even better because you don't have to talk them into it. Just aim the Nagan [pistol] and shout, 'Lie down!'. . . take care of your business and be off."

"We're deep inside East Prussia where we're chasing after the Prussians so bad the feathers are flying. Our boys have already tried out all the German women."[20]

## AGAINST THE MADNESS OF REVENGE: ALEKSANDR SOLZHENITSYN AND OTHER SOVIET OFFICERS

Aleksandr Solzhenitsyn, then a young captain in the Red Army and a committed opponent to such outrages, describes the entry of his regiment into East Prussia in January 1945: "Yes! For three weeks the war had been going on inside Germany and all of us knew very well that if the girls were German they could be raped and then shot. This was almost a combat distinction . . . ."[21]

In his epic poem *Prussian Nights,* Solzhenitsyn gives a more compelling description of the wanton arson and murder:

We've hit him good and hard, the foe!
Everything's aflame. —Night quarters?
We'll have to spend it in the snow.
Oh, well, that's bad. But all the same,
We've given *them* a tougher time:
The whole district sees a dawn
The like of which it's never known! . . .
To flame the work of centuries turns,
Fire is weaving, fire is lashing,

Above my head it burns and burns. . . .
In Neidenburg conflagrations shiver
To shards old masonry's good stone.
The town's a chaos; in a fever
Of acquisition our pursuit takes it. . . .
Twenty-two Hoeringstrasse.
It's not been burned, just looted, rifled.
A moaning, by the walls half muffled:
The mother's wounded, still alive.
The little daughter's on the mattress,
Dead. How many have been on it?
A platoon, a company perhaps?
A girl's been turned into a woman,
A woman turned into a corpse.
It's all come down to simple phrases:
*Do not forget! Do not forgive!*
*Blood for blood!* A tooth for a tooth!
The mother begs, "Soldier, kill me!"
Her eyes are hazy and bloodshot.
The dark's upon her. She can't see.
Am I one of theirs? Or whose? . . .
A pram that's been abandoned,
                    Blue,
            Lace trimmings, too:
    "Look, a little 'un.
    Still, he's a German!
He'll grow and put a helmet on.
Deal with him now, d'you think?
The order from Supreme Command
Is *Blood for Blood!* Give no quarter!". . .
And then they shot the housewife first,
Spattering with blood the carpet's pile.
The husband was bedridden, ill:
They cured him with a carbine burst.
Only the nephew, a young boy,
In a flash managed to escape
—Out of the window and away
Over the fence with a leap! With a leap!
    Like a wild creature,
    Like a little hare,

Across the field toward the wood
Running, ducking, dodging aside.
The whole troop, nearly, rushed from the road,
Firing anyhow, in pursuit:
　"I'll get him!" "Winged him!" "He's down!"
　"He's away!" "—Shoot! Shoot!"
　"Ah, the brute,
He's got away. Well, when he's grown . . ."[22]

Solzhenitsyn vocally opposed this indiscriminate violence against civilians and was consequently arrested, then banished to a gulag. Major Lev Kopelev and other Soviet soldiers and officers suffered the same fate for their insistence on humane treatment of the German civilian population.[23]

Among them was Captain Ivan Pavlovich Petrash, even though his brother, nephew and son-in-law had been killed in Leningrad. His other nephew and his nephew's brother had been hanged in Odessa. Petrash fought in Leningrad and in the Ukraine. In 1945 he was in Neustadt, Upper Silesia, serving as deputy city commander. He received an order that all Germans between the ages of 17 and 55 years were to be deported to forced labor camps in the Soviet Union. He disobeyed the order and instead sent the citizens off to help with the local harvest. Time and again he saved German women and girls from the outrages committed by other Soviet soldiers, and later by Polish soldiers and civilians.

Johannes Klein, an Upper Silesian who survived the Soviet occupation, remembered Petrash with respect: "He belongs to those few bright lights which shone in that otherwise blackest night. He was not the only one, but since he was given great authority by virtue of his office, his humanity, magnanimity and clear perception of justice and injustice did much good for a community numbering in the thousands."[24]

Unfortunately, such officers were in a distinct minority. Most sought booty and momentary pleasure.

Of course, it must not be forgotten that the local Nazi Party officials bore a large part of the responsibility for the catastrophe, often blocking timely evacuation of civilians until it was too late to proceed in an orderly manner. Innumerable columns of people in flight were thus overtaken by the advancing armored divisions. People were mowed down by gunfire or outright flattened by tanks rolling over them. Considering the dangers of flight, many refused to leave their homes. And many never survived the period of Soviet occupation. Representing countless similar fates is the story of Marie Neumann of Pomerania, quoted here verbatim.

## The Testimony of Marie Neumann[25]

*On Sunday, March 4th, around noon, the shooting became more distant. Our SS, which was last fighting in the Lucknitzer Woods, had withdrawn and the Red Army occupied the city (Baerwalde). My husband, who was sitting just outside the public shelter, must have realized this. He became very nervous and insisted that we give ourselves up. So he asked me for a white kerchief. I cried and didn't want to give it to him as I feared for his life. My husband got angry with me, saying I was the one who was losing her nerve, and that he had thought he could expect more from me, that I would be brave. So I pulled myself together and gave him the kerchief. My husband then left the shelter with two Poles and came back just a short time later. All of them had their watches taken away, and had orders to get us all out of the shelter. We all came outside hearing that usual shouting of the order "Urri, Urri." We had to line up and go to the commandant. We asked for permission to take our belongings with us, which was allowed; and then we were ordered not to go to the commandant but to our houses. We were accompanied by Soviet military police. Along the way we were met by Soviet cavalry, all Mongols and Asians; they were frightening to look at, and we became even more scared. Two military policemen accompanied us, my sister and her children, into our house. Right away one of them gave us his field flask of vodka, and each of us had to drink two glasses. Then we each got a piece of sausage which we ate even though we had no appetite. We were glad that they were so friendly, and had no idea of what was to come. My husband then told me to go back to the shelter with him to get the rest of our things. My sister begged to go along so she and her children wouldn't have to stay behind alone in the house with the soldiers. My husband agreed. He and my sister said I would get along with the soldiers better anyway. You see, my sister was very frightened with all this. She put her suitcase in my room and asked me to keep an eye on it. As soon as they left the house I was raped for the first time by the two Soviets. When they were finished with me, one of them opened my sister's suitcase and my brother-in-law's golden watch, which lay right on top, found its way into his pocket. Then for the first time I got a pistol pressed against my chest. Then my loved ones came back, my husband white as the plaster on the walls, my sister covered with blood.*

*But she had escaped from what they wanted her to do in the shelter because my husband had stepped in. But now she became the victim of these a thousand-times-accursed military policemen.*

*After that one of them went off while the other stood guard in front of the house, continuously calling out to the passing Russian troops, bringing in several hordes of seven to ten men, one group after another. My sister was on one side of the house with her seven-year-old daughter, and I was on the other side with her two other children and my husband. Someone had pressed a burning candle into his hand. My sister and I were raped again and again. The beasts lined up for us. During this time one of the military policemen held the door shut. I saw this because I was finally left alone before my sister was. Once she and her daughter both screamed in a most unnatural way, so that I thought they were being killed; and I wanted to go over to them when the policeman standing guard burst into our room and knocked my husband to the ground with his rifle. My niece Ilschen was crying and threw herself on my husband while the boy and I held the policeman's arm crying loudly, otherwise he would probably have killed my husband.*

*When we were finally granted a little peace and my husband had regained his senses, my sister came over to us and begged my husband to help her, asking, "Karl, what's going to happen to us?" My husband said, "I can't help any of you; we're in the hands of a mob, not soldiers, and they're all drunk out of their minds." I said, "Karl has to hide himself or they'll beat him to death; they've already beaten him half to death." My husband agreed with me and wanted to hide, but Grete held him back and begged him to think of her poor children. My husband then answered: "Grete, I just can't help anybody, but I'll stay with you; all we can do is hide, all of us, out in the hayloft." No sooner said than done. But just as we were climbing up into the loft, three men appeared; since there was snow outside, they had seen our tracks. We had to climb down; the two little girls were kissed and their mother raped again. She and her children cried so that it broke my heart. She cried out desperately: "O God, O God, why is this happening?" The men left, and my husband said: "They're going to kill me, they're going to kill all of you, and what they'll do to the children you can well imagine." My husband said that hiding now made no sense, we don't have any time to do it. I said: "Everybody get up there. I'll lock all the doors and they'll have to break them down first," hoping that it would give us the time to hide ourselves. But I had forgotten in the excitement that the yard gates had been broken down already because we had been* closing them whenever we could. We had just gotten into the loft when there came a howling and yelling of rabble in our yard, shooting like crazy into the ground, and then they came after us. It had gotten dark in the meantime and they had flashlights. They were civilians and some military wearing cornered hats with pompoms. What happened next I can barely write down, the pen sticks in my hand. They hanged us all in that hayloft, from the rafters, except for the children. The mob strangled them by hand with a rope.

Later I was told by the people who had taken shelter in the Hackbarth family's cellar on Polziner Street that they had heard our unnatural screams, even down in the cellar; but no one had the courage to come for us, they were all fighting for their own lives at the time. I came to on the floor, lying next to my loved ones. I didn't know yet what had happened to them, although I had a good idea, it was the details I lacked. Because I was first thrown to the floor when the mob caught us, hit on the head and raped, after which I was hanged. I had lost consciousness immediately. Later I heard voices. I was lying on the floor, four men kneeling around me. They said, "Frau komm," and when I tried to stand, I fell down at once. Later I found myself in the yard being held up by two men. They took me inside and laid me on a bed. One of the four men, a civilian, a Pole, stayed by me and asked: "Frau, who did?" I said: "The Russians." Then he hit me and said: "Russians, good soldiers. German SS, pigs, hang women and children." I fell into a fit of crying; it was impossible to stop. Then the other three came back in, but when they saw me, they left my apartment. Shortly thereafter a Russian came in carrying a whip, constantly yelling at me. Apparently he wanted me to be still, but I just couldn't. So he hit me once with the whip, then kept hitting the side of the bed. When that didn't work, he gave up and left my house. Then I heard voices in front of the house and got more scared than I was ever before or since. Seized by a cold panic I ran out to the little creek next to our garden, where the geese used to swim. I wanted to drown myself and tried for a long time until I was faint. But even that didn't bring my life to an end.

How I got through all this I don't know to this day. In any case someone had hauled me out of the creek. When I regained my senses I made my way to Fraulein Bauch's room on the ground floor of Schmechel's, the shopkeeper. Dear God how I was freezing *because there were no windows or doors left in the place, and my clothes were wet; it was the night of March 4th to 5th and there was still snow and ice about. After a while I saw there was a bed in the room, so I laid down thinking I was alone in the place. But I quickly saw that someone had been sitting at the table and was now standing up, coming over to my bed, and, oh no, it was a Russian. Suddenly my whole miserable plight came before my eyes. I cried again and begged him if he wouldn't please shoot me. He shined a flashlight into my face, took off his coat and showed me his medals, saying that he was a first lieutenant and that I need not be afraid. He took a hand towel down from the wall and began to rub me dry. When he saw my throat, he asked: "Who did?" I said, the Russians. "Yes, yes," he said, "Was the Bolsheviks, but now not Bolsheviks, now White Russians; White Russians good." He then took his bayonet and cut off my panties, whereupon I again was ready to die, for I didn't know what to expect anymore. He rubbed my legs dry; but I was still freezing and didn't know what I should do if I had frostbite. But then he took off my wedding ring and put it in his pocket. He asked me where my husband was, and then raped me in spite of my miserable condition. Afterwards he promised to send me to a German doctor. I was happy about that, but then I remembered there were no more German doctors in our area.*

*Shortly after he left four 18- to 20-year-old Russians appeared. Totally drunk, they pulled me out of bed and raped me in an unnatural way. In my condition I wasn't able to do more and fell beside the bed, so they kicked me with their boots, getting me just in the worst spot. I fainted again. When I came to, I crawled back into the bed. Then two more such bums showed up, but they left me alone as I was more dead than alive. I learned back then how much a human being can endure; I couldn't talk, couldn't cry, couldn't even utter a sound. They hit me a bit, which didn't matter to me since I couldn't feel anything, and then left me alone. I fell asleep out of sheer exhaustion.*

*When I awoke very early next morning, I realized again where I was. I quickly noticed an open wardrobe door, and inside was a dress. There was also a shirt and some underwear. So even though the things were much too small, I put them on; what was left of my clothes was still wet. I had to put the dress on leaving the back unfastened, to make it fit. There were no stockings to be found; mine had been wound up* so tight they were like bones. Then I was visited by the Russians again. First one who apparently thought the room was empty, because when he saw me in bed, he left the room immediately. He came back with three more men; that first one wanted to hit me, but the officer wouldn't let him. So the first man pointed to the Hitler portrait on the wall which was full of bullet holes, and he said I was a Hitler fascist. I said, "No! This isn't my house." He said, "Come! Go your house!" I had to walk ahead of them to my house and must have been a pretty sight. When I got there I saw a truck parked in front, and Russian soldiers were loading my slaughtered livestock into a car. The soldiers almost laughed themselves to death when they saw me. They indicated to their officer, their fingers tapping their heads, that I was probably crazy, and when four female soldiers appeared, they wanted to shoot me. But the officer didn't permit it. He asked about my neck, and I said, "Russian soldiers; my husband, sister, children, too." When he heard the word children, he was shocked. I asked him to come to the barn with me but he didn't want to, and I wasn't allowed to go back either. So I asked to go to the commandant. He agreed at once with that and sent a soldier with me. But when we got to the corner by Kollatz, he indicated to me that I should continue along Neustettiner Street by myself. There were several men already in the marketplace, clearing things away. When I got to the butcher, Albert Nass's place, a Russian soldier told me to go in: Commander's Headquarters.

Inside the courtyard I saw three farm wagons filled with Poles, men and women, all in new clothes. Leather chairs and other furnishings came flying out the windows and the Poles leapt at them in a frenzy. Then I saw the Pole who, if I'm not mistaken, was there when my family was murdered; in fact I'm sure he was there, just when they were picking me off the floor. He was the one who hit me when I said it was the Russians who did this. I went over to him and asked to see the commander. He said, "No speak German". "Yes you do," I said. "You were there at my place yesterday, and you could speak German quite well." He screamed at me: "I there, I not there, so what. You keep quiet!" A Polish woman came over and said: "What you want, German sow? Commander not for Germans. Commander for Poles. I take whip and chase you away!" As I was about to leave the courtyard, a Russian soldier said, "German woman! Stairs there, go up." I was immediately made a prisoner for my effort, locked into a room with others.

When evening arrived, it was hell itself. One woman after
another in our group was hauled out. The shoemaker's wife, Frau
Graf, who was in her last month of pregnancy, was taken, also a
woman from Wusterhausen, and the Peters' daughter Frau
Schmidt. They were driven away by some soldier. The women
screamed as they were being forced into the car, and the prisoners'
room was full of screaming. Our nerves were raw. Then we heard
the motor revving up, the Russians shone searchlights into the
room through the window, so bright that several women screamed
out that they were using flame throwers against us. The children
cried miserably; it was horrible. Toward morning the women
came back. Two came into the room and collapsed; the other
woman was raped once more by the door before they let her in.
They came to get me once during the night. I was taken into the
slaughterhouse and assaulted on a feather bed right on the soil.
When I came to, my neighbor Herr Held was crying over me. My
neck had swollen so much over the past hours that I had trouble
moving my mouth, and I was spitting blood.

The next morning the Polish "gentlemen" wanted a turn with
us, but none of us moved to go along. That one certain Pole,
always the worst of the lot, had wedding bands on every single
finger, top to bottom. (Oh, it's so disgusting to think back on all
this.) The next night was not much better than the first. We still
had not been given anything to eat or drink. Toward morning
some Poles came and said that we had to go to Neustettin. There
the commandant of Neustettin would give us the necessary papers
so that we could return to our homes. They drove us out into the
street and said that whoever didn't come would be shot that night.
The butcher, Herr Nass and his family had come back home in
the meantime. People like us were also coming out of the houses
across the street. I felt so miserable that I didn't want to go. Frau
Loewe said, stay with us and come what may, we won't make the
march either. But all the others, especially the Peters family,
talked me into it because they were afraid I would not live to see
the next morning. Peters had a hand cart with him; it had
bedding in it. He told me I should grab onto the back end and
they would pull me along. Gradually the march began to move;
up front were the wagons filled with Poles decked out in their new
finery, followed by Poles on new bicycles, then at the rear, the

*Germans. A procession of misery which exceeded by far the lines of foreigners that had come through Baerwalde during the war.*

*In the evening we arrived in Neustettin. The Russians directed us to the officers' villa. We had still had nothing to eat, and were not permitted to cook anything ourselves even though food was available there, and we could smell cooking odors. The night was quiet. The next morning two Russians came and ordered us to accompany them to the commander, get our documents, and then go home. We had to leave our baggage out in the street where women with small children also had to wait, as did old people and those badly wounded in the war. We were taken around the church to, I think, Fischer Street. We were taken into a house. No hearing. Twenty-eight people from Baerwalde were there. Women left, men right, crowded in a room where many other Germans waited. The room was about 12 meters square; two beds with mattresses, a closet wardrobe, a chaise lounge, and a chair. Whoever couldn't find a place to sit had to stand. We got something to eat on the third day. On this third day we were counted, whereby the victims for that night were looked over. When the beasts came in the night, of course no one wanted to go, so there were some horrible scenes.*

*After several days we were ordered to assemble out on the street. We Baerwalders had not yet been registered, and since no one could understand why we were not on the list, they just gave us false names and registered us as Hitler fascists.*

*We were taken to the courthouse. There we were written up as Party members. In my case the female interpreter wrote Nazi Women's Association. When I said that was wrong, she forbade me to speak and said: "Other woman said about you." (The next day the list of names was missing again, anyway.) After getting written up a Russian took us into the courthouse basement and locked us up. No furniture in the cell, the floor made of red brick, the windowpanes smashed. Besides us Baerwalder women there were a few women from Neustettin, two of them not very cordial. The next morning during toilet break, which always took place in the wood shed under the watch of Russians, men and women together, we saw furniture being piled up in the forecourt. We stole a few things so we'd have something to sit on in that crowded room. At night ten of us women were always taken out to peel potatoes, a bathtub full, in the kitchen. Then out to the wood shed to fetch*

firewood, guarded by an interpreter. I was always one of those chosen. What that cost me in nerves no one can ever know.

On the third day another transport was leaving, this time with
Herr Nass, Herr Kaske and Frau Nass. The Nass's daughter and
niece had to stay, which was quite painful for them. We were then
moved to the lodgings of the prison officers. Here we had to lie on
the floor again, but at least it was a wooden floor. There were
several sick people in the room, among them persons with dysentery. But then we all had diarrhea, open sores and the like. We
never were given water to drink or wash with, so we all stank, to
say the least.

On the following night the devil himself was on the loose. The
Russians came in continuously. They pushed their way between
the sleeping women, kicking us in the darkness with their boots
and spurs. It didn't matter to them which woman they got hold
of. The niece of Herr Nass, a girl of 16, got a saber drawn across
her throat because she refused to let herself be taken, and from the
backside at that. And the brave girl did not even make a sound;
she did not allow herself to be used. Unbelievable things were
happening at night on Fleischer Street as well. It was so bad that
the men who were imprisoned with us in the same room said that
they couldn't take it any more, what the Russians were doing to
us women; so they made a formal complaint; and we heard that
the men were beaten for this, so we said to them: "If they would
just stop beating you!" So our pain was double, our own fate and
our men's. After this terrible night we were made to leave the
prison and assemble in the courtyard; we were then given bread,
the first bread we had seen in weeks. The bread was our provision
for the march to Hammerstein. That bread smelled as good as
cake, but no one among us could eat right away; we wanted it to
last. We came to a fine villa. They had to force us to go in because
we thought it was a brothel.

There we were finally interrogated. And since I had never been
political or had anything to do with the Party, they let me go. I
had to make the frightening trip home by myself. It took me five
days. Partisans were still fighting in the woods. I came to a village
where I wanted to spend the night, but most of the houses were
occupied by Poles; they wouldn't give lodging to any German.
Other houses had dead bodies in them. The Germans kept a low
profile out of fear. Or they stayed together, several families in

groups. But despite this precaution it was the same story: "Frau, come!"... along with robbery and looting. Poles who would drive by me in wagons would call out: "Cherman or Polaka?" If one answered German: "German nix gut." And to underline that they'd hit you around the ears with the horsewhip. Around the edges of the forests I saw starving stray livestock wandering aimlessly. And there were still innumerable bodies laying everywhere. Many had their skulls bashed in, and women all had their dresses pulled up. It was as bad as the outward journey. When I was near Grabunz, I met some women and men from Baerwalde. They were there to bury the bodies that lay along the road. I learned from them that they had buried my loved ones in our garden the previous evening. That is how long they had been hanging in the hayloft. That made my homecoming still harder. My house had been ransacked just after my family was buried; everything was in the church waiting to be carted off to Russia.

When I finally got to my house, I wanted to die. All the windows were smashed, the shutters were lying out on the road. So were the rest of our clothes. The right gable was partly destroyed by a bomb or gunfire. In the house all the remaining furnishings were smashed. Tables and chairs were turned over. Whatever had been in cupboards and closets lay on the floor, covered with water and filth. I was incapable of even going into the house; I just leaned in the doorway and wished I were dead. The mason Hackbarth's family found me like this. Herr Hackbarth took me to his house where he asked me: "Are you Frau Neumann? Or perhaps not?" A few days later I met my sisters-in-law on the street, Frau Marquardt and Frau Holz, and they asked me the same question.

The Hackbarths suggested that I go to the city commander, register, and demand my sewing machine and bedding be returned. My feather bed, clocks, mirror, sofa, radio, etc., were in the church, as I mentioned above. I was afraid to go, but the Hackbarths said that the commander is a just and good man. So I gathered my courage. A woman interpreter took my request to him. He asked where I lived. I answered, in the house where he had yesterday given permission for my family to be buried. When he asked me how they died, I said, "Russian soldiers, half civilian, half military had done it." "When did this happen?" I said, "On March 4th toward evening." And I began to cry, whereupon he said that if I don't stop he'll have me locked in the cellar; and that he would hear no more from me, for the German SS had acted like this in Russia. And that soldiers with cornered hats would be Polish, same with the civilians. It was Polish partisans who had been in the prison camp at Neustettin; on March 4th they came through Baerwalde; they were the ones who did it, he said. I could have my sewing machine back, if I pledged to sew for the command office, and no more. I agreed. I got no bed, and whatever else I needed I was told to get from some other house. And since my house was kaputt I was ordered to find some other place to live and then let him know where I was. I took the former abode of Mayor Stoeckmann at the Hackbarths. A Pole, who had been carting beds into the church, brought my sewing machine to me. His name was Smuda, and he would later often bring meat, lard and the like because he took pity on my fate. For my sewing work I received no provisions or pay, just the usual bread, one loaf per week, now and then two pounds of syrup. Two months later the commander's wife and child arrived. Then it got better for me; I received provisions and they were also very nice to me, in contrast to the women interpreters. After an additional two months the entire Polziner Street as well as some homes on Schirlitz Street were confiscated by the Russians. The civilian administration left, and military headquarters were installed in its place. My duties were transferred to the military commander, I had to sew for him, too; and since the Hackbarths had to give up their house, I moved back into mine.

Herr Hackbarth was once again the one who helped me get permission to move. But then the Eastern Poles came into our town, too. They were similar to or even worse than gypsies. Totally ragged, barefoot, they went to the Polish city government, got a piece of paper, and drove us Germans from our homes. They came to my home twice, but couldn't do anything since it was requisitioned by the Russian commandant. At that time I had to keep several women busy. There was Frau Hampel, Frl. Witzker, Frl. Schellin; and Frau Schellin cooked for us. We had to sew for some 200 men of the Batallion Staff which was stationed in Greifenberg, Altdamm and Baerwalde. Things went well during this time. We got the same provisions as the Russian soldiers. Besides, we always had to cook something extra special for the officers in the evening, and therefore we managed to get some *extra for ourselves. We were protected from any possible Russian or Polish mistreatment; we even had passes that stated we were working for them. Captain Koslowski was especially good and fair with us. Whenever we came to him with some need he would look after us like a father. If it hadn't been for the Polish civilians, we'd have no complaints at all from this time. The German civilians who had no commandant protection had a far sadder time of it. The Polish militia behaved like crazy people; the Poles in the occupied houses no better. Women would often come to me, asking that I report things to the commander. Once a woman named Frl. Minna Schulz came to me, her whole face black and blue, hit by her Polish overseer. Still she was put in prison. I reported the matter to the GPU (Soviet police) and got her some help. A merchant's wife named Manske from Patzig asked me to report that she was being raped each night by Russians, along with her elderly mother-in-law. The commander told me a few days later that it was indeed Russians who had been laying a telephone cable near there. And there were many more such women. If the Poles needed a workforce or additional hands, the Polish militia would search house-to-house. Without permission the house, barn, even the garden was searched, and if someone was found, they would be marched off to forced labor.*

*I was often asked about the perpetrators of my family's deaths. I answered now that it was the Poles. Because of this I was frequently cautioned by Germans that the Poles wanted me arrested. On November 5th, 1945, Frau Stegemann went to Frl. Schellin and actually told her that she had heard the Poles were going to arrest me and take me to a camp early next morning. I told this to one of the Russian officers, that maybe he would help me get across the Oder River, as I had been promised if I worked hard. He said they couldn't do that any more, since the Poles were now making the decision as to who could leave. I thought I would go mad, hoped someone would shoot me, but the Russians stayed quiet. That night we were all afraid. For three months since the confiscation of her house, Margot Schellin slept in my room. At around midnight there came a tapping at the window. "Open up!" Margot wrapped her arms around me tight, and we shivered like aspen leaves. Someone knocked again, and I soon lost my fear, for it was the same four knocks the Russians always used when there was work to be done at night. And, O miracle, it was the*

*Russian officers. They told me to quickly pack up my bedding and*
*some clothes, that at ten to eight in the morning a Russian car*
*would be waiting to take me to the refugee camp at Muencheberg*
*near Berlin. They had gotten information that the Poles were*
*going to pick me up at 8 A.M. Margot was instructed not to tell*
*anyone, not even a German; she was to say that Frau Neumann*
*went to Greifenberg, a new sewing assignment. On November 6th*
*just after 7 A.M. a Russian ambulance pulled up with six GPU*
*soldiers inside; and then we were off. Since they had to guess their*
*way as to which bridge or road to take, it was two days before I*
*was in Kuestrin; and at the beginning of February I was taken*
*across the Oder. There, too, everything had been completely*
*looted. . . .*

Frau Neumann survived her ordeals, eventually traveled farther West,
leaving the Soviet occupation zone and settling in Burgwedel, near Hannover.
She was able to start a "new life," remarry and have a daughter—possibly the
only thing to do for one whose life had been so mangled by fate and who would
not commit suicide, as so many other rape victims did.

Yet it remains a wonder that anyone could endure so much suffering without
losing her reason. The story told by Marie Neumann, among thousands of others
filed in the Eastern Documentation section of the German Federal Archives,
testifies to the capacity of the human being to withstand profound anguish and
despair following the murder of husband and children and constant physical abuse.

## The Testimony Of Erika Trakehnen

Such experiences gave rise to many personal expressions of that pain and
humiliation. When I asked another expellee woman, Frau Erika Trakehnen,[26]
how she had coped with the horror, she gave me a collection of poems written
by her and entitled *A Mother's Thoughts,* reflecting the same feelings as those
of Frau Neumann:

At home and yet not at home—
the Russians come every night—
Dear God I beg You
send me sleep, make me forget. . .
Forget. . .
Shamed, degraded, tread upon
I pull myself up with newer wounds.—

Forget. . .
Is a woman's lot to be so treated—enslaved?
Is there no law, no justice?
Forget . . .
Is this our life, is this our pain?
To serve nothing but the lusts of men?
Forget . . .
Is that all we are here for?
I once stood with Peter at the altar . . .
Forget . . .
For I have children, children to protect.
We have our husbands, though not with us now . . .
Forget . . .
I beg of You, God, make me sleep and forget
And judge not my life based solely on this. . . .

The official Soviet version of this period winds like a superfluous, decorative arabesque around the perimeter of hard reality. Professor Boris Telpuchovski of the Institute for Marxism-Leninism in the Central Committee of the Communist Party of the USSR pretended in his *History of the Great Patriotic War:* "The Soviet soldiers, the pupils of the Communist Party, behaved humanely toward the German people." Indeed, Russian historians of the post-Communist period will have to come to grips with these events and with Stalin's overall responsibility.

Ambassador George F. Kennan summarized the horrors committed by the Soviet soldiers with greater accuracy:

> The disaster that befell this area with the entry of the Soviet forces has no parallel in modern European experience. There were considerable sections of it where, to judge by all existing evidence, scarcely a man, woman or child of the indigenous population was left alive after the initial passage of Soviet forces; and one cannot believe that they all succeeded in fleeing to the West . . . . The Russians . . . swept the native population clean in a manner that had no parallel since the days of the Asiatic hordes.[27]

Remarkably enough, ignorance of this chapter of history is worldwide, and by no means limited to the Russian Federation and the former Soviet republics and satellites. With the notable exception of persons like George Kennan and Robert Murphy, few Americans have hitherto addressed these events.

To excuse historical ignorance of this aspect of the war by saying that, after all, the Germans got what they deserved is not only poor rationalization but morally unacceptable. Of course, in domestic politics selective indignation is a familiar device used by politicians who will not apply the same measuring stick to similar events. In history it is apparently not different.

## REFUGEE FLIGHT ACROSS THE BALTIC SEA

Fear reigned in the East. Millions fled west in panic, knowing what had occurred at Nemmersdorf, Metgethen and countless other localities. By comparison, the German populations of the Rhine and Ruhr regions, equally threatened by foreign occupation, did not flee east but stayed in their homes and largely welcomed the British and Americans as liberators. At least for them the war was over.

Anglo-American and French soldiers did commit numerous abuses against the civilian population, but no massacres occurred as in the East.

In January 1945 the situation in the eastern provinces of the Reich grew more desperate by the hour, and soon the land routes to the West were cut off. Hundreds of thousands therefore attempted to trek to the Baltic Sea with hopes of evacuation over sea.

The long trek to the coast was marked by bitter cold, and yet the refugees had wished for even lower temperatures; for although the ice over the Königsberg Bay (Haff) was thick, it was not always strong enough to support their heavily laden wagons. Approximately 24 km of ice had to be crossed in order to reach the port of Pillau on the Nehrung land strip on the other shore of the bay. Sometimes this stretch could be negotiated in six to eight hours, sometimes it took days. Exhaustion and freezing temperatures claimed many victims.

What made the scene all the more ghastly were the Soviet planes executing low-level assaults, mercilessly mowing down refugees with machine guns or bombing the ice to crack and weaken it, causing many wagons to sink in the waters of the Haff. The refugee trek was an unimaginable struggle against desperation.

It has been estimated that half a million refugees traveled over the frozen Haff in order to reach Pillau or other harbors on the Nehrung strip.

Getting to the Nehrung peninsula did not mean safety, however, for air attacks continued to take more and more lives. Of course there were military targets in Pillau, as in any harbor. On the other hand, a military justification cannot be made for keeping such a harbor under constant fire, when it was no secret that tens of thousands of civilians waited there for evacuation.

Admiral Konrad Engelhardt had been entrusted with the rescue operations. On the order of Fleet Admiral Karl Dönitz, he placed every available ship in the eastern Baltic at the disposal of the evacuation effort. A total of 790 vessels took part in the enormous venture, including naval and merchant ships as well as smaller private craft. Often convoys of as many as 12 ships would depart at one time. This Baltic Operation eclipsed in size and difficulty the otherwise memorable British naval evacuation at Dunkirk in May 1940.[28]

It proved to be a relatively secure method for getting many refugees to the West. However, the few catastrophes at sea were so sensational that an impression has emerged that the sea evacuation was as ghastly as the treks.

The best-documented tragedy is the sinking of the *Wilhelm Gustloff* on January 30, 1945. She was sunk by Soviet submarine *S-13* under the command of Captain A. I. Marinesko. The *Gustloff* sailed from Pillau along the Pomeranian coast for Mecklenburg, carrying more than 6,000 refugees. Several hours at sea, she was shaken by three successive explosions and began at once to list to port. The Baltic seas were rough, the decks covered with ice, the lifeboats frozen fast and the water temperature was 2 degrees Centigrade (35.5 degrees Fahrenheit). Despite the fact that other ships were in the vicinity and that the *Gustloff* took 90 minutes to sink, barely 1,100 persons were saved.[29]

## The Testimony of Harry Weller

Captain Harry Weller, one of the catastrophe's survivors, tells his story in a statement given to the author, written in the third person.

> *On January 29, Corvette Captain Wilhelm Zahn made a report to officers on board regarding the situation in the Baltic Sea. He explained that the Bay of Leningrad was controlled by the German Navy. The Gustloff would not have to deal with enemy ships or submarines on its journey west. Air attacks were another matter. For this reason the ship was to be equipped with a few more anti-aircraft guns before departure. Moreover, the trip would begin just before nightfall as additional precaution. German air security was guaranteed for the next day. The Gustloff was adequately staffed with technical personnel. Chief Engineer Franz Loebel had already reported the engines at ready as of January 27. Cabins, salons, the drained swimming pool as well as some vestibules were crowded with wounded and refugees. One*

concern of the ship's officers was its stability under this load, and the fact that sufficient numbers of life vests and other rescue apparatus had to be provided. Only 12 of the Gustloff's 22 lifeboats still hung on their davits. With the assistance of the Naval Service Bureau in Danzig-Langfuhr, the ship was quickly provided with rescue and lifesaving gear for 5,000 persons. Twenty naval smallboats were lashed to the sundeck, and an adequate number of marine life rafts were stacked there as well. Ship's officers frequently repeated instructions to the passengers on the procedures in case of emergency. Safety drills were held as was practice in sealing off bulkheads. On January 29 the ship's officers ordered four naval tugboats and a pilot for the departure from harbor.

In those days of January 1945, Gotenhafen [today Gdynia] was the last major gateway to the West. The great passenger liners *Deutschland, Hamburg, Hansa* and *Wilhelm Gustloff* were packed full with thousands of refugees. The ships were to make the sailing westward in a secured convoy. On departure day, January 30, 1945, it appeared that only the *Hansa* and *Gustloff* would sail in mutual escort. But then this also fell through when the *Hansa* developed engine trouble and was forced to drop anchor in the outer harbor. Then, instead of four naval escort vessels, the *Gustloff* was assigned two, the Torpedoboat *Loewe* and Decoy Vessel *TF-1*. Captain Weller was not satisfied with this reduced, weak security; he demanded greater protection from the Commanding Admiral for the Eastern Baltic. The protest was rejected, and he was ordered to set sail.

According to an informal purser's report, handed on a sheet of paper to the First Officer, at time of sailing the *Gustloff* carried 918 naval officers and marines, 173 civilian crew members (stewards, cooks, technical personnel and seamen), 373 Women's Naval Auxiliary personnel, 73 critically wounded (soldiers incapacitated by plaster casts, lying on stretchers)—these last being situated in the ballroom beneath the bridge—as well as 3,121 registered refugees. Just how many additional people got on board through special contacts or illegal means was never known. A total of 4,658 persons was actually counted. But there were certainly several hundred more people on board.

The *Gustloff* followed the Torpedoboat *Loewe* and Torpedo Decoy *TF-1* at 12 knots. The seas grew steadily rougher and sprayed across *the forecastle. Snow showers alternated with periods of clearing. Near the peninsula of Hela the TF-1 reported via semaphore: "Taking on water through weld seam." The escort had to be relieved and took off for Hela. The light Torpedoboat Loewe took over security by itself. In the heavy seas the men of the torpedoboat did their best, protecting the great passenger liner as well as they could. A full flanking screen was now out of the question. Then broke the night of horror.*

*Sailing in total blackout the ship steered westward, seas grew heavy. A coded radio message informed the Watch that a minesweeper group was headed our way. The course steered by the Gustloff was in an outward lane of the Baltic free of mines; but the area had to be constantly swept for floating mines dropped by aircraft. For a number of reasons the Gustloff was not able to use the mine-free lane closer to the coast. Because of the approaching minesweeper group, the Gustloff turned on its running lights. The topmast lanterns and the red and green flank lights could be dimmed by means of a rheostat. Rixhoeft was passed around 1930 hours, meaning that by 2100 the lighthouse at Stilo should be athwart and to the rear. During the war all lighthouses on the German coast shone only at certain intervals known to every sailor. Here, too, on the Pomeranian coast the officer-of-the-watch knew when it was possible to take bearings on the ship's position. The navigation officer would correspondingly record the position on the chart. The ship steamed through the sea, the wind had let up a bit, visibility was good, now and then the moon would peer through the clouds. It was getting colder; the seaspray was freezing on the decks and rigging.*

*It was 2100 hours. Aback and off the port side the lighthouse at Stilo blazed briefly. The navigation officer took a bearing and recorded it on the chart. Captain Weller was on duty; in the chart house at 2104, he confirmed the position of the Gustloff for himself. As Weller was leaving to return to the bridge, indeed just as he was standing in the door frame of the chart house, a shockwave ran through the ship. The power of the blow was such that the captain was thrown upward, hitting his head on the top beam of the door frame. Mines, he shouted, and with a single leap he was at the engine telegraph pulling the indicator to STOP. We've come upon a minefield, was his first thought. The shrill signal bells were sounding from the telegraph when a second and third powerful jolt seized the ship. The vessel immediately listed* to port; a glance over the bridge rail revealed the bow was going down, already awash. Due to the downward angle, people on the foredeck were pouring into the sea, unable to save themselves. All lights on the ship went out. A Russian submarine had lain in waiting and dealt the Gustloff three torpedo hits. The engines stood still, ship's telephones and loudspeakers were mute. The bulkheads began to burst, steel braces tore, the ship listed more and more to port. Captain Weller skidded to the portside bridge nock, pulled himself up and climbed to the bearing deck. "Fire red!" he roared at the signalmen. "Fire everything we've got!" Luckily the signals were spotted by several ships. Escort Loewe saw the red flares, heard our SOS and was able to relay it. The ship's officers, the captains and Corvette Captain Zahn were all on the bridge, and all agreed: The ship is lost! Every man for himself. Deploy all lifeboats; do everything possible!

The battle for the lifeboats began. The regular crew got some of them into the water; other boats slipped and smashed on the surface. Women and children first was not possible. Passengers on the upper decks could save themselves more readily; the rising waters floated the lashed naval smallboats and life rafts, which saved a great many. There began in crazed panic a fight between life and death. Sailors were trying to get the lifeboat launching mechanisms working at the davits, hard work because windlass and tackle were caked with ice. The crush of people was too great. Escape from the lower decks was impossible. All staircases were at such an angle that they could not be climbed. A few engine room personnel managed to reach the sundeck via emergency ladders located in ventilation ducts. The wounded soldiers in the Grand Ballroom, the Women's Naval Auxiliary members in the swimming pool, all were lost. The death struggle of the Gustloff lasted 90 minutes. Captains Weller, Koehler, Corvette Captain Zahn; the navigation officer, radio officer and signalmen were all still on the bridge. The ship was now listing 20 degrees, the bow sunk lower and lower, the stern rose ever higher. Suddenly the ship's emergency lighting came on everywhere. The emergency diesel had been started by unknown hands. The Gustloff continued to slowly sink. With the last of the now-floated life rafts, persons on the bridge, bearing deck and sundeck saved themselves. Several younger sailors did not heed the advice of older seamen, donned life vests and jumped overboard, intent on swimming to the drifting lifeboats and rafts. They were never heard from again. The Gustloff sounded its demise with the long-drawn, depressing howling of its distress siren. Escaping air in the ship's interior had automatically set it off. The lights went out. Torpedoboat Loewe circled the sinking ship, capturing in its searchlight the thousandfold struggle for naked existence. The Loewe's commander and crew saved whom they could, taking as many on board as absolute capacity allowed without itself sinking under the weight. At the site where the Gustloff finally went under teemed crowds of shipwrecked humanity. They swam, clung to wreckage, rafts, lifeboats and smallboats. Two hours had now passed.

Torpedoboat T-36, security escort to the heavy cruiser Admiral Hipper, was first to reach the site of the tragedy. It immediately began to assist in rescue operations. The T-36, under the command of Captain Robert Hering, threw rope ladders over the side, lines and hawser netting, by which the stronger survivors could clamber on board. Lifeboats and rafts in the hands of seamen could maneuver alongside the T-36, the others still drifted. As chance would have it, Corvette Captain Zahn, Captain Petersen and Captain Weller were all rescued by the T-36. Zahn and Weller had first been picked up from the rafts by two different lifeboats, as were many others drifting about. During the approximately two hours in which this ghastly scene was played out, most of the shipwrecked could not reach a rescue vessel. Captain Weller recalls helping pregnant women and wounded soldiers out of lifeboats onto the deck of the torpedoboat. The crew of the torpedoboat gave their all in the effort to save as many as possible. Weller reported immediately to Commander Hering on the bridge of the T-36. Hering asked Weller if he had not known that, since midday, January 30, enemy submarine activity had been reported off the Pomeranian coast. This naval dispatch had somehow not reached the bridge of the Gustloff. Otherwise different course and sailing conditions would have been imposed. . . .

A Russian submarine was indeed situated in front of the Libau harbor. . . . Soaked to the skin and exhausted, the shipwrecked men now aboard the T-36 were taken to dry off. Weller and Zahn were in the wheelhouse of the T-36 when the radar room gave Commander Hering the position of a submarine via a device quite similar to today's radar. Distance 1400 meters, bearing 15 degrees portside. Great *danger for ships and their human cargo. All around were boats, rafts, people. Commander Hering had no choice but to pursue the enemy sub: Full speed ahead, prepare depth charges! A terrible yet necessary decision under these circumstances. It was the only chance for those already saved. Many of the boats and rafts alongside the T-36 capsized when the torpedoboat started up. The detonations of the depth charges also brought a quick end to many still stranded on boats and rafts. Horrible! Throughout and after the depth charge attack, the Russian sub could not be traced. Twenty minutes more were spent at the site of the sinking. Then Commander Hering had to give up, his boat was loaded with survivors beyond safe maximum. . . . The T-36 headed for Sassnitz on the island of Ruegen. . . . According to the Commander's list, 564 Gustloff survivors were on board the T-36. During the trip from the night of the sinking until noon next day many died anyway. Exhaustion, shock, exposure overtook the rescued people crowded into the crewmen's quarters, the mess and the boiler room. One rescued doctor was nevertheless able to assist pregnant women and help bring new life into the light of the world. The hospitals in Danzig had shipped their pregnant patients, even those in labor, on the Gustloff. The ship's officers were aware of this as well as of the presence of many critically wounded.*

*Doctors had been ordered on board to care for these people. The Torpedoboat Loewe also had to break off its rescue operation for lack of space on board. It sailed for Kolberg with 252 survivors. Naval and commercial vessels that later crossed the zone of the sinking were able to rescue more people from rafts and lifeboats, even some still clinging to wreckage. Besides the nearly 800 people saved by the two torpedoboats a further 300 were saved in this manner. The number saved, 1100, stands in marked contrast to the number drowned, over 5000.*

A few days after sinking the *Gustloff,* Soviet Captain A. I. Marinesko went on to sink the hospital ship *General von Steuben* on February 10, 1945, sending 3,500 wounded soldiers to a sandy grave.

Probably the most devastating catastrophe at sea occurred on April 16, 1945, when Soviet submarine *L-3* under Captain V. K. Konovalov torpedoed and sunk the freighter *Goya.* It was later calculated that the vessel held somewhere between six and seven thousand refugees, of whom only 183 persons survived.

In spite of these disasters, the German navy and merchant marine continued their rescue missions until the last days of the war. The Hela peninsula on the

Nehrung land strip was overflowing with refugees, still hoping for rescue. On May 6, 1945, 43,000 refugees were picked up. Two weeks after the capitulation ships were still landing in Schleswig-Holstein loaded with refugees. The last ship to reach the harbor had ended its journey with a smashed compass. Yet thousands of civilians and soldiers remained on Hela, beyond any further evacuation west. All the soldiers and many civilians were taken into Soviet custody, sent into forced labor in the Soviet Union and often never heard from again.

The following excerpt from the unpublished memoirs of a naval officer, then assigned to help coordinate evacuations through the Danzig Bay, reflects the mood of the period.

## The Testimony of Corvette Captain A.

*An icy east storm raged over Gotenhafen [Gdynia]; and a Red storm broke on the night of January 11-12, 1945. Russian tank formations thrust rapidly to the west, then fanned out toward the Baltic Sea, driving the civilian population before it, when not actually rolling the crowds down. The Russians soon reached the Baltic at Cranz and cut off the land strip connection to Memel.*

*Minesweepers brought the first refugees from Pillau: women whose children had frozen to death in their arms. Gotenhafen spilled over with refugees arriving by train, in organized evacuation treks, and alone on foot. . . .*

*In the meantime, the first ships designated for refugee evacuation had arrived. The beautiful Hapag steamer Arcona was considered over capacity with 8,000 on board; on its next trip it would cram 12,000 souls!*

*Ten days later the Russians were already in Elbing and on the Haff. Refugees attempted to flee over the ice. Thousands drowned, froze to death or were killed by strafing aircraft. . . . The brave seamen of the coast guard landed on the Nehrung, stood in ice water up to their stomachs and lifted women and children on board. Gotenhafen meanwhile had been completely evacuated. Looters were shot and left to lie where they fell as warning; railway freight cars filled with masses of frozen-dead refugees stood on the harbor tracks.*

*Toward the end of March, the Russians broke through in the direction of Zoppot. Danzig and Gotenhafen were subjected to constant bombardment; divebombers were unhindered in their work above the two cities. Danzig fell on March 27. An attempt to evacuate wounded from the military hospital met with disaster. As we later found out, some of them had been shot in their beds. The remaining technical personnel from the Schichau Shipyards at Elbing and Danzig were able to save themselves on one of the last ships to sail from Danzig. They would later build a new existence for themselves in Bremerhaven. One could see the fires from the sea. With heavy heart I have since recalled that winter night lit by the full moon, a night when I was overwhelmed by a sad foreboding. Whoever had not fled could dodge capture in the Vistula delta, which, since several levies had been blown, was a bit more defensible.*

*The most terrible scenes were played out from the end of March 1945, during the embarkations at the Hela pier. If attack planes appeared, the transports would weigh anchor and cast off the shuttle boats, for the wrecks of two hospital ships, clearly marked as such per international norm, lay upon the northeast shore of Hela. Their example was always in mind. Many children became separated from their mothers, only to be reunited years later after painstaking search by the Red Cross. On some days more than 100,000 people swarmed on the Hela peninsula, waiting for the next convoy out. After each air attack it was no small task to get the dead safely buried. Troops had indeed become so indifferent with all the deaths that a dead woman and her bleeding child just did not count anymore.*

*A ferryman arriving with wounded from Pillau complained that half of them died along the way. One was shocked to see the long rows of wounded wrapped in their paper bandages—for a long time there had been nothing better. Still the order remained: All wounded must be evacuated!*

*The Russians shelled the beloved old naval town of Pillau from three sides. Women and children kept crawling out from under the debris waiting to be evacuated. The icebreaker East Prussia, decked out with antiaircraft artillery, arrived in Hela harbor from Königsberg/Pillau with "His Honor" Gauleiter [District Leader] Erich Koch on board. He ostentatiously demanded a security escort, for he was on his way to see the Fuehrer. The Admiral of the Eastern Baltic, Admiral Burchardi, refused a special escort. Moreover, his chief-of-staff quickly dispatched 100 East Prussian refugees to the icebreaker's berth, where they were chased away by the bodyguard of this scoundrel Koch. He also delayed the timely evacuation of a large encampment of ca. 2,000 young women from Samland. Koch is also responsible for the fact that General Friedrich Hossbach,*[30] *probably the most competent troop leader in this phase of the war, who was just in the process of reestablishing the link to West Prussia south of Elbing, was relieved of his objective and ordered by Hitler to make a 180-degree about-face.*

*There was little in the way of provisions on Hela. After the arrival of experienced Kurland veterans, horses were slaughtered. Bleeding gums were cured by chewing pine needles while taking a leisurely walk along the train tracks in the warm April sun. Farther trackside one would encounter couples embracing in the tall grass, hardly put off by the general apocalyptic mood of defeat nor by Russian grenades rocketing overhead from the Oxhoefter Kempe.*

*On May 8, 1945, 70,000 more men were again shipped off the peninsula, while in the west weapons were already still. . . .*

*Approximately 1.5 million refugees and more than 700,000 soldiers were evacuated from East and West Prussia by the navy in collaboration with the brave merchant marine. The remaining population, which was overtaken by the Russian advance, went through hell.*

And so it ended in the north. Farther south, in Silesia, people fled along the land routes primarily in organized treks, some by train. Many headed for Dresden.

## THE DESTRUCTION OF DRESDEN

Until the beginning of 1945, Dresden had been spared aerial bombing raids. There were no troops and hardly any military targets in the old baroque city—if at all the railway station, which was not only an imposing building, but also a hub for rail traffic. Many thought that Dresden would remain unscathed owing to its cultural significance, as Paris or Rome had been spared.

No fewer than 200,000 Silesian refugees were in the city—the number is probably much higher—on Tuesday, February 13, 1945.

At around 10 in the evening a thick cloud of British bombers appeared over Dresden. The first assault wave was over by 10:21. The city was on fire. A second wave followed at 1:30 A.M., February 14. A total of 1,400 British planes took part. And as if that were not enough, at 12:12 the following afternoon 450 American planes disgorged their bombs upon the city.

All told, 3,000 tons of incendiary and high-explosive bombs were dropped. It is estimated that 135,000 persons died. Approximately 400,000 were left homeless. Ironically, this air attack did not accelerate the end of the war by even one day. The massacre was militarily meaningless.

## The Testimony of Johanna Mittmann

Johanna Mittmann, a courageous woman from Upper Silesia, at that time employed by the Reich Railroads, was entrusted with the evacuation of the children of railway employees. She had left Oppeln (Upper Silesia) bound for Dresden. After the war she emigrated to the United States, where for more than 35 years she has been an American citizen, residing first in Wisconsin and now in Florida. She recalls the day of the German Hiroshima:

> *Totally exhausted, we finally reached Dresden, together with 78 boys and girls. The youngest was eight weeks old, the oldest were 14-year-olds Franzl Butter and Franzl Friebe, who later came to live with his grandmother, as his parents were never found.*
>
> *The children were tired when we finally arrived in to Dresden; they cowered on the seats or huddled on the floor. When would we be picked up? Who would receive us at the station? It seemed impossible that someone in Dresden could find these dead-tired children in this mountain of people, on this night, when the city held between 2 and 3 millions crowded together. . . . But since we had the two children of the Reich Railways Councillor Meyer in our group, and since Herr Meyer knew the number of the train we took to Dresden Central Station, he would surely find a way.*
>
> *Suddenly there was a strange crackling in the air. Endless searchlight streams danced like tinsel above the suddenly darkened city, and crowds of people pushed and poured out of all the stalled trains, hoping, if necessary, to reach one of the air raid shelters in time. It would be virtually impossible to keep the 78 children together under these circumstances, so we decided to wait in the train, pairing off the children so that an older one looked after a younger, in case we had to leave the coach anyway. I had a loud whistle with me and made it clear to the children that in case we were separated, they should immediately run to where they last saw me or listen for the whistle. It was then that the first*

*bombs hit, and quite close to us. Every one of us was sitting or kneeling on the floor of the coach praying to heaven that we stay safe. Since I myself believe deeply in the mediation of the Divine Mother, we endlessly repeated the prayer: "Help, Mary, the time is come; help us, Mother of Mercy." The impacts all seemed to be so near, and unavoidable . . . screams from outside . . . and then on our train platform crevices were rent open, spewing flames. Yes, I saw two older men running for our coach suddenly engulfed in the flames. Aren't those up there, dropping these bombs, human beings just like us? Could a fellow human have actually issued orders to kill us so indiscriminately? The frightened prayers of the children would break one's heart . . . and our little group was just a small fraction of that mankind crowded together in Dresden.*

*I had wrapped Klaus Dietrich in a blanket and carried him on my back, for the barely nine-year-old boy suffered from pneumonia; we had difficulty getting him from Buchwald to Zillertal, but we couldn't leave him behind to fall into the hands of the Russians, not after I had seen examples of their barbarism. Then it was suddenly over, and in a few minutes the children stopped whimpering and went to sleep. I must have slept myself, for when I awakened with a start, the train had been moved to the west bank of the Elbe River, the railway station on the opposite bank a single sea of flame. Although the heat was now oppressive we could not leave the coach, for the second assault had just begun. It was before 3 in the morning. I thought it might be a good idea to crawl with the children down to the river. But the water was burning! I heard later that the first wave had dropped only incendiary bombs, while in the second, high-explosive and naphtha bombs were dropped in order to get at the people in shelters! People who had sought safety in the parks were killed by falling trees. . . . Eventually the feverish Klaus had to have some water or at least a wet head cloth. When at long last the assault was over we climbed out of the coach, which, miraculously, did not even have one damaged window. We marched like a mother goose and her goslings to find some water or even something to eat, and to get out of the stifling air which blacked out the now risen sun.*

*We finally came upon some Red Cross people who stared at us wide-eyed: living people from among all those dead, and such a neat and orderly little group! We had avoided the iron rails, which were still hot. A few of us had blisters from stumbling onto hot metal. But how many times we were asked: "How did you get here?" And it was hard to believe that we had gotten out of there, the Dresden Central Station, a place where not even a mouse could have survived; and then, dying of thirst, came here begging for water.*

Johanna Mittmann tells us of survival. She spares us, however, the descriptions of horror as whole blocks of homes burned from ground floor to the rafters and the manner in which individual people staggered out from this furnace.

Burning torches. They screamed, as only people in the throes of death can scream. They collapsed. Hundreds of burning, screaming human torches collapsed and were silent. And they were followed by more, and still more. None of these survived their torment. . . . The street was strewn with corpses, torsos hung from the twisted trees. . . . People wandered numbly about. One man ran as if possessed into a burning house which came crashing down upon him. . . . The conflagration created a firestorm. Hissing and spitting it stoked the flames. . . .[31]

## GERHART HAUPTMANN AT DRESDEN

Gerhart Hauptmann, the Silesian novelist from Agnetendorf in the Riesengebirge, was in the Weidner Sanitorium nearby in Dresden-Loschwitz. From this vantage point he saw the burning city, and in tears he said: "At that moment I wanted to die." Later he wrote:

A person who has forgotten how to weep, learns how once more at the sight of the destruction of Dresden. Till now, this clear morning star of my youth had illuminated the world. I know that there are quite a few good people in England and America, to whom the divine light of the Sistine Madonna was not unknown, and who now weep, profoundly and grievously affected by the extinguishing of this star.

And I have lived to see personally the destruction of Dresden by all he hells of Sodom and Gomorrah, caused by the airplanes of the enemy. As I use the words "live to see," that still seems like a miracle to me. I do not take myself seriously enough to believe that Fate has kept this horror in store expressly for me and in this very spot in the world that is almost the dearest of all to me.

I am very close to leaving this life and I envy all my dead comrades of the spirit who did not live to see this horror.

I weep. Do not take offense at the word "weep"; the greatest heroes of antiquity, Pericles and many others, were not ashamed of it.

From Dresden, from its wonderfully sustained nurturing of the fine arts, literature, and music, glorious streams have flowed throughout all the world, and England and America have also drunk from them thirstily.

Have they forgotten that?

I am nearly eighty-three years old and stand before God with a last request, which is unfortunately without force and comes only from the heart: it is the prayer that God should love and purify and refine mankind more than heretofore—for their own salvation.[32]

What makes the massacre especially repugnant is the fact that it was carried out in cold blood. The crimes against women and children committed in Nemmersdorf and Metgethen discussed earlier occurred in conjunction with an infantry offensive and its attendant high losses among the soldiers. Those who perpetrated rape and other excesses against the civilian population were caught up in the psychosis of battle, in the delirium of fear or of alcohol, intoxicated by the roaring sound of guns, enraged by the vision of dead comrades. In contrast, the carpet bombings of German cities by the Anglo-American formations were terrorist attacks, ordered by deskbound trigger-pullers. The "area bombing" policy of the Strategic Bombing Command was based on a decision made by the British War Cabinet on February 14, 1942, whereby operations from that point forward would aim at breaking the morale of the enemy civilian population, in particular the industrial labor force.[33] Approximately 600,000 civilians were victims of this bombing terror.

# 4

# Allied Decisions
# on Resettlement

Each army, whether Axis or Allied, bears its own responsibility for the outrages committed by its soldiers during the war. This applies to the crimes of the Soviet army in eastern Germany as well as the destruction of Dresden by the Anglo-American bomber formations. The responsibility for the decision to uproot and resettle millions of human beings, to evict them from their homes and spoliate them—and this as a quasi-peacetime measure—is also a war crime for which individuals bear responsibility, even if many would still hesitate to put the correct label on the crime and its perpetrators.

In August 1941 British Prime Minister Winston Churchill and American President Franklin Roosevelt met aboard ship in the middle of the Atlantic Ocean; they agreed to a declaration of their common goals, which were proclaimed on August 14, 1941, two days after the conclusion of the conference.

Similar to President Wilson's Fourteen Points in World War I, this Atlantic Charter represented a general catalog of principles, a program for peace. The most important of its eight points were:

1. The Anglo-American Alliance seeks no aggrandizement, territorial or other.
2. The Alliance desires to see no territorial changes that do not accord with the freely expressed wishes of the peoples concerned.

3. The Anglo-American Alliance respects every nation's right to self-determination.

4. The Alliance will endeavor . . . to further the enjoyment by all states, great or small, victor or vanquished, of access, on equal terms, to the trade and to the raw materials of the world which are needed for their economic prosperity.[1]

The other nations of the anti-Hitler coalition were quick to accept the principles of the Atlantic Charter, including the Soviet Union and the governments-in-exile of Poland and Czechoslovakia.

## THE FIRST ALLIED RESETTLEMENT PLANS

Dr. Eduard Benes, president of the Czechoslovak government-in-exile, worked tirelessly during this time to prepare the expulsion of Sudeten Germans from Czechoslovakia.

In a 1942 lecture given at Manchester University, England, Benes said that "[t]ransfers are a painful operation. They involve many secondary injustices. The framers of the peace settlement could not give their consent unless the transfers were humanely organized and internationally financed."[2] Benes made reference to the population exchange that had taken place from 1923 to 1926 between Greece and Turkey. It had been accomplished under the supervision of the League of Nations in accordance with the terms of the Treaty of Lausanne of 1923. Some half million Turks were exchanged for twice as many Greeks.

The initial target in Benes's plan was the Munich Agreement, which he wanted declared invalid, so that the borders drawn in 1919 by the Treaty of St. Germain might be reestablished. British Prime Minister Neville Chamberlain had already informed Benes during the Munich crisis in 1938 that, in case of armed conflict, Czechoslovakia "could not be reconstructed in her frontiers whatever the result of the conflict may be."[3] Even after Hitler had violated the Munich Agreement by his illegal occupation of Bohemia and Moravia, Chamberlain reiterated in a Birmingham speech that the borders determined by the 1919 Treaties of Versailles and St. Germain had been unjust.[4]

While Benes was attempting to set up a government-in-exile and to have the Munich Agreement declared null and void, the U.S. Ambassador to France William Bullitt commented in a letter to President Roosevelt, dated September 16, 1939:

Benes arrived in Europe intending to set up a "provisional government of Czechoslovakia." . . . both the French and British took the
position that they had refused to admit that Czechoslovakia had
ceased to exist as an independent state. . . . they could see no basis
for a Benes provisional government, except Benes's desire to place
himself at the head of something again. Moreover, nearly everyone
in political life in both France and England considers that Benes is
an utterly selfish small person who, through his cheap smartness in
little things and his complete lack of wisdom in large things,
permitted the disintegration of his country.[5]

Yet, the escalation of the war, in particular the collapse of France, lent support
to Benes's plans. Thus, after the fall of the Chamberlain government, the new
British Foreign Minister Anthony Eden moved away from the Chamberlain
concept when he declared in August 1942: "At the final settlement of Czechoslovak
frontiers to be reached at the end of the war, they [the British Government] will
not be influenced by any changes effected since 1938." Eden further informed
Benes that "his colleagues in the Cabinet agree in principle to resettlement."[6]

This first official acceptance of the principle to uproot hundreds of thousands of people was followed, in the summer of 1943, by its acceptance by
Roosevelt and Stalin.

Further provisional decisions concerning the expulsion of Germans were
made at the Tehran Conference in December 1943. Since Stalin wanted to keep
the eastern half of Poland, which he had occupied according to the terms of the
Molotov-Ribbentrop Pact of September 1939, some form of compensation had
to be found for Poland. East Prussia would be ceded to Poland, perhaps Upper
Silesia as well. The German populations would have to be removed. Whatever
Poland would lose in the east, it could gain back in the west. Churchill
demonstrated his thoughts on a Poland shifted westward with the help of three
matchsticks. Stalin was quite pleased.

To be sure, the Poles were upset with the prospect of losing eastern Poland,
including Lvov and Vilnius; but the Western powers sought to make this more
palatable by offering logistical support. President Roosevelt promised his help
in a letter to the prime minister of the exiled Polish government in London,
Stanislav Mikolajczyk: "If the Polish Government and people desire in connection with the new frontiers of the Polish state to bring about the transfer to and
from territory of Poland of national minorities, the United States Government
will raise no objection, and as far as practicable, will facilitate such transfer."[7]

In a speech before Parliament on December 15, 1944, Churchill was more
specific: "Expulsion is the method which, so far as we have been able to see, will

be the most satisfactory and lasting. There will be no mixture of populations to cause endless trouble. . . . A clean sweep will be made. I am not alarmed by these large transferences, which are more possible in modern conditions than they ever were before."[8]

However, the experts in the Foreign Office and State Department viewed the situation somewhat more cautiously. Their main concern was that resettlements be kept to a minimum. There was support for the idea that only "selective" resettlements be carried out, which would not begin until several months after the war had ended. There was talk of a "Population Transfers Commission," which would regulate the conditions and modalities of resettlement. With the memoranda of several experts at hand, Roosevelt and Churchill went to Yalta.

## THE CONFERENCE AT YALTA

At the Conference at Malta on 1 February 1945, British foreign minister Anthony Eden and the American Secretary of State Edward Stettinius warned against extending Poland's western border to the Oder River, for that would require extensive population resettlement.[9] They advocated only the cession of East Prussia, which meant a resettlement of 2.5 million Germans. At Yalta (3-11 February 1945), Stalin and his hard-line foreign minister Vyacheslav Molotov, however, demanded the border be extended to the Oder and western Neisse, which meant a resettlement of 11 million people—9 million inhabitants of the eastern German provinces and 2 million from Old Poland and the Warta District. Churchill and Roosevelt knew what was going on. They were not duped by the Soviets, as some believe, because allegedly they had no geographic sense of the situation. They knew full well that there were two rivers with the name Neisse; they were unmistakably against a border on the western stream.

Churchill was opposed to Stalin's designs because, in his own words, "a considerable body of British public opinion . . . would be shocked if it were proposed to move large numbers of Germans."[10]

Marshal Stalin responded by claiming that most Germans in the disputed territory had fled their homes in advance of the Red Army. This statement was false. At least 5 million Germans still lived there, even though some 4 million had indeed fled.

Churchill insisted that any resettlement must be undertaken in proportion to the amount of German territory that Poland could be reasonably expected to absorb safely and the number of Germans who could be transferred to Germany. "It would be a pity to stuff the Polish goose so full of German food that it died of indigestion."[11] Roosevelt also protested, stating there could be no justification for pushing the border to the western Neisse.[12]

The decision was tabled. First the war had to be won. A fateful decision was made, however, on February 11, 1945. The discussion revolved around reparations for the Soviet Union, which demanded the use of German work forces. This was nothing more or less than trade in human beings, slavery. But the statesmen had coined a euphemistic phrase for it: "Reparations in kind."[13] Churchill and Roosevelt agreed to the Soviet demand.

The Yalta agreement on "reparations in kind," the effects of which are herein described beginning on page 113, clearly demonstrates the complicity of Roosevelt and Churchill in this slave labor program, even though no German civilians were deported for such purpose to the United States or Great Britain. The Anglo-Americans nonetheless incurred a historically far-reaching responsibility in that moment when they decided upon Germany's future.

## THE POTSDAM CONFERENCE

Cecilienhof, a palace built from 1913 to 1917 in the surroundings of the city of Potsdam, just outside Berlin, for Crown Prince Wilhelm von Hohenzollern, was the meeting place for the Potsdam Conference. From July 17 through August 2 it was host to the heads of government from the United States, Great Britain and the Soviet Union, the "Big Three" as they were called. France had not been invited.

It was not, however, a peace conference similar to the 1919 Paris meetings; in fact, it was more a preliminary conference called to solve only the most urgent problems. The war was not yet over. The United States and England were still fighting Japan, and the Soviets were supposed to join in.

There were other decisions more important to the Big Three than the fate of the eastern Germans. For the Soviets there was the all-important question of reparations, which was related to the drawing of any new boundaries. How could the Soviets demand reparations from the rich industrial region of Upper Silesia, for example, if this province was to be taken away from Germany and given to Poland?

Churchill and the new American president, Harry S Truman, declared themselves against an expansion of Poland to the Oder and western Neisse rivers. At most, Poland should assume territory up to the Oder, but no farther. At the fifth meeting, on July 21, 1945, Truman pointed to the German character of the Oder and Neisse regions and to the 9 million Germans resident there. Stalin responded as he had five months previously in Yalta: Many of the Germans had been killed in the war and the rest had fled the region. He emphasized that not one single German lived in the territory to be transferred to Poland. American Admiral William Leahy called over to the president: "Of course not, the Bolshies have killed all of them."[14]

The Polish government, invited to air its thoughts on the Oder-Neisse boundary, spoke of only 1.5 million Germans resident in the disputed area who would "voluntarily withdraw, as soon as the harvest is in."[15]

No one thought to mention the fact that, although nearly five million Germans had fled before war's end, more than one million were now trying to return. In the summer of 1945 the actual number of Germans living in the Oder-Neisse region reached approximately five-and-a-half million people.

The Anglo-Americans were reckoning on a narrow margin of resettlement, certainly not out of any sympathy for the Germans, but for practical considerations of postwar reconstruction. For as the Allies conquered Germany, they also assumed responsibility for feeding and housing the German population.

Thus, Churchill demanded that any resettlement remain limited in scope. He even suggested that some of the German refugees who had fled to the West be given permission to return to their communities east of the Oder and Neisse. As Churchill said, the Britons would have serious moral doubts about any comprehensive population resettlement. "We could accept a transfer of Germans from Eastern Germany equal in number to the Poles from Eastern Poland transferred from east of the Curzon Line—say two or three millions; but a transfer of eight or nine million Germans, which was what the Polish request involved, was too many and would be entirely wrong."[16]

Despite these objections, the Western allies finally agreed to the transfer of the eastern Germans. They could have said no and waited to see what happened, but they wanted to avoid any breach with the Soviets. Sir Denis Allen, a member of the British delegation, recalls:

> We were then all too well aware—and to a degree hard to picture in retrospect—of our ignorance of what was really happening in Eastern Europe and still more of our inability to influence events there.
>
> If experience of the Nazi era and of war had engendered a certain numbness and indifference to human suffering, it had also bred new hope that, against all the odds, the wartime alliance might be consolidated into a workable system of post-war collaboration in Europe and in the world at large. So there was a widely shared determination not to press concern over events in the East that we could not prevent, to the point where it might maim at birth the

Control Council and the United Nations; if hopes were to be frustrated, let it be the Russians and not ourselves who were seen to be responsible.[17]

Another member of the British delegation at Potsdam, Sir Geoffrey Harrison, today refers to the psychological factors, particularly to the notion that conferences must be successful. "We wanted Yalta and Potsdam to be regarded as success stories. It wasn't until 1947 that we gave up on the idea that every conference must have a happy ending."[18]

James Riddleberger, a member of the American delegation and chief of the Central European Section in the State Department, takes a similar view.[19] He knew of a memorandum by George Kennan that had warned in vain of the dangers involving a border on the Oder and Neisse. He also supported the American Secretary of State James Byrnes, who had gone so far as to complain about the lack of perseverance among the other members of the American delegation: "I regret being unable to see any sign of decisiveness on our part. Everyone seems to accept as fact that we will give in on the Oder-Neisse question. Nevertheless I am still attempting to bring some backbone into this matter."[20]

After some initial opposition from the Western allies, Article IX of the Potsdam Protocol regarding the German-Polish border and Article XIII regarding the so-called transfer of Germans were adopted. The first paragraph of Article XIII reads: "The Three Governments having considered the question in all its aspects, recognize that the transfer to Germany of German populations, or elements thereof, remaining in Poland, Czechoslovakia and Hungary will have to be undertaken. They agree that any transfers that take place should be effected in an orderly and humane manner."[21]

This represented neither an incentive to nor a flat acceptance of expulsions. The article was actually intended to bring then on-going expulsions under a regulated procedure. According to paragraphs 2 and 3, the Allied Control Council in Berlin was to determine when and how many Germans were to be resettled. Until then a moratorium on expulsion was in effect.

Sir Geoffrey Harrison, member of the British delegation, drew up the draft of this article. On August 1, 1945, he informed the Foreign Office:

> The Sub-Committee met three times, taking as a basis of discussion a draft which I circulated. . . . The negotiations were not easy—no negotiations with the Russians ever are. . . . We had a great struggle, which had to be taken up to the Plenary Meeting. . . . [Soviet subcommittee member] Sobolev took the view that the Polish and Czechoslovak wish to expel their German populations was the

fulfillment of an historic mission which the Soviet government were unwilling to try to impede. . . . [The American subcommittee member] Cannon and I naturally strongly opposed this view. We made it clear that we did not like the idea of mass transfers anyway. As, however, we could not prevent them, we wished to ensure that they were carried out in as orderly and humane a manner as possible.[22]

The moratorium was ignored in any case. The expulsions continued just as before, and during the conference itself.

Four years previously point 2 of the Atlantic Charter had promised no territorial changes that did not meet the freely expressed wishes of the affected people. The Sudeten Germans, East Prussians and Silesians were not asked if they wanted to leave their 700-year-old homelands. They were thrown out.

During a debate on February 23, 1944, in the House of Commons, Anthony Eden had expressed the following view:

There are certain parts of the Atlantic Charter which refer in set terms to victor and vanquished alike. Article 4 does so. But we cannot admit that Germany can claim, as a matter of right on her part, whatever our obligation, that any part of the Charter applies to her.[23]

Churchill made a similar remark on May 24, 1944: "There is no question of Germany enjoying any guarantee that she will not undergo territorial changes if it should seem that the making of such changes renders more secure and more lasting the peace in Europe."[24]

The noble principles were thus repudiated, as Labour MP John Rhys Davies acknowledged on March 1, 1945 before the House of Commons: "We started this war with great motives and high ideals. We published the Atlantic Charter and then spat on it, stomped on it and burnt it, as it were, at the stake, and now nothing is left of it."[25]

# 5

# Expulsion and Deportation

## THE EXPULSION FROM CZECHOSLOVAKIA

Until the end of the war there was practically no German flight from Czechoslovakia, for the country had remained extensively in German hands. In fact, several hundred thousand refugees fled Silesia for the safety of the Sudetenland.

In the last days of April, in western Bohemia, the American Third Army under General George Patton crossed over the ancient German-Bohemian border. By May 4 the Americans had taken the Egerland, but they stopped along the Karlsbad-Pilsen-Budweis line. The American occupation, perceived as liberation by most Sudetan Germans, was not accompanied by looting, rape or hangings.

On May 5, 1945, a Czech rebellion broke out in Prague. The memories of the infamous Nazi massacre at Lidice in 1942 and of the Gestapo terror inspired acts of revenge taken against German soldiers and civilians.

An armed group of Czechs succeeded in occupying the studios of Radio Prague 2. The slogans broadcast were "*Smrt Nemcum*" ("Death to Germans") and "*Povstani! Povstani!*" ("Revolt!"). As with most revolutions, the mobs raged out of control, leading to brutal murders. German soldiers were disarmed, tied to stakes, doused with gasoline, then set on fire as living torches. German civilians were arrested, mistreated and humiliated. Several thousands were killed.

Following the German capitulation on May 8, wild expulsions of ethnic Germans began. May 30, 1945, saw an estimated 30,000 residents of Brno chased headlong from their homes. The London *Daily Mail* reported:

> Shortly before 9 P.M. young revolutionaries of the Czech National Guard marched through the streets calling on all Germans citizens to be standing outside their front doors at nine o'clock with one piece of hand luggage each, ready to leave the town for ever. Women had ten minutes in which to wake and dress their children, bundle a few possessions into their suitcases, and come out on to the pavement. . . . Once outside they had to surrender all jewelry, watches, furs and money to the guardsmen, retaining only their wedding rings. Then they were marched out of town at gun-point to the Austrian border.
>
> It was pitch dark when they reached the border. The children were wailing, the women stumbling. The Czech border guards pushed them over the frontier towards the Austrian border guards. Then more trouble started. The Austrians refused to accept them; the Czechs refused to readmit them. They were pushed into a field for the night, and in the morning a few Romanians were sent to guard them. They are still in that field, which has since been turned into a concentration camp. They have only the food which the guards give them from time to time. They have received no rations. . . . A typhus epidemic now rages among them, and they are said to be dying at the rate of 100 a day. 25,000 men, women and children made this forced march from Brno, among them an Englishwoman who is married to a Nazi, an Austrian woman 70-years-old, and an 86-year-old Italian woman.[1]

There are few photographic documents covering this phase of the tragedy. One photograph was taken on May 8, 1945, by an American army photographer. It carries the caption: "American medics of the 16th U.S. Tank Division treat German civilians beaten by angry Czechs."[2]

Pilsen was occupied by the Americans. This granted the population a certain measure of protection against arbitrary brutality. In point of fact, American soldiers were repeatedly called to intervene. Robert Murphy, political adviser to the American military government, reported several times on the interventions of American commanders who "in friendly but firm fashion, have told the local Czechs that certain acts simply cannot be tolerated in the name of humanity, but even so, ruthless evictions have occurred on a sufficiently large scale to antagonize many of our troops against the liberated Czech people.[3]

The greater part of Czechoslovakia east of the Karlsbad-Pilsen-Budweis line was occupied by the Soviet army. Brutal attacks on the German civilian population occurred in these regions; moreover, with the approval of the Soviet army, the Germans had been expelled long before the Potsdam Conference had in principle sanctioned forced resettlements.

For example, the Germans of Boehmisch-Leipa in northern Bohemia had been expelled on June 14, 1945. The expulsion order permitted the expellees to take 100 Reichsmarks with them. Gold, silver and other valuables had to be surrendered. It is interesting to note that physicians, veterinarians, pharmacists and skilled laborers were not included in this first order. They were not expelled until some time later.

Not far from Boehmisch-Leipa lies the town of Aussig on the Elbe River (Usti nad Labem). On July 31, 1945, there was an explosion at the cable works. Some Czechs suspected sabotage on the part of the ethnic Germans. A bloodbath followed. Women and children were thrown from the bridge into the river. Germans were shot dead on the street. It was estimated that between 1,000 and 2,500 people were killed.

The British ambassador at Prague, Philip Nichols, who was shocked to learn of these atrocities in Aussig/Usti, telegraphed the Foreign Office:

> Two British born women who were present in Usti at the time confirm these allegations, adding that the acts in question were probably the result of a spontaneous outburst by Czech hooligans. The mass of the Czechoslovak population, they say, was deeply ashamed of this outburst the following day. It is this kind of behaviour which increases the determination of the American troops in Bohemia to insist on "fair play even for Germans"; and this attitude, in its turn, causes friction with the Czechoslovaks who charge the Americans with German sympathies. The Americans are reported to be collecting a dossier of Czechoslovak excesses with photographs.[4]

In 1990, after the "Velvet Revolution" brought President Vaclav Havel to power, a plaque was placed on the Usti bridge in remembrance of the German victims of this massacre.

In the first months following the end of the war, Germans were defenseless against criminal acts and harassment. In a U.S. Army report dated October 27, 1945, we read:

Frau Anna Hruschka, a Sudeten German from Kottiken, 7 km north of Pilsen, stated that a Czech soldier and several Czech policemen forced their way into her house, confiscated all dishes, crystal and clothing, after first beating her sister and brother-in-law. That same day Frau Hruschka went to Pilsen in order to report the assault to the Czech Army Headquarters on Klattauer Street. After she had returned home two police officials came and took her to the local precinct station in Kottiken. There she was asked about her trip to Pilsen and levied with a fine of 1,000 kronen, because she had gone to Pilsen without permission and had not worn the yellow armband. She was so badly mistreated that she fainted. One eye is still bandaged to this day, the other is blackened.[5]

Similar tales of harassment may be found in the 40,000 eyewitness reports filed in the Eastern Documents section of the German Federal Archives.

But there are many thousands of stories not contained in the archives. Of the 12 million eastern Germans who survived flight or expulsion, only a small fraction recorded their experiences in writing. It was not until after the publication of the first books on the expulsions, or the broadcast of a film on the subject, that many expellees felt motivated to tell their stories. It was thus that I received a letter from Frau Else Seethaler of Ludwigsburg, telling of war's end and expulsion.

## The Testimony of Else Seethaler

*When the Front was getting ever closer on May 8, 1945, we fled from the Russians toward the west. (I was not yet 18.) Dive bombers attacked the refugee treks—there were many dead and wounded, and nobody cared about them. Our journey ended near Melnik. People by the thousands were driven into freight cars— whoever refused was shot. They were being deported to forced labor in Russia.*

*We managed to make our way to the estate of Prince Josef von Lobkowitz. Once there we were arrested and locked into storage sheds, treated and guarded like hardened criminals. 90% of the people were elderly, women and children. We were told that since we were civilians, we would be getting papers and could then go home. But we ended up living there for 13 months under cata-strophic circumstances. We worked the fields from early morning into the night. "Food" was available in the pig troughs. Whoever sought to collect something edible while out in the fields was immediately shot (for stealing from the Czech people!!!).*

*Night after night we were handed over to the Russians—what they did with us is indescribable! Whitsuntide '45 I was knocked unconscious by a Russian officer and hauled off. . . . We were so starving that we even ate the poisoned rodent bait we were supposed to put around the potato stacks. One old man went to get a tin can from the garbage pile and was caught by a guard. We all had to line up and watch as the old man was made to strip to the waist, stand on one leg with his arms raised and shout: We thank our Fuehrer—all the while he was whipped until, covered with blood, he collapsed. Such incidents were the order of the day.*

*When we were deported, our train carried one car filled with food, but when we transferred at the German border, that car went back with the freight train; not one of us was given any of the promised provisions.*

*Here is a copy of our deportation order:*

> *County Administration Commission in Friedland.*
> *Deportation Order!*
> *Herrn, Frau . . . .*
> *You are hereby ordered to prepare yourselves and your entire family for departure from the territory of the C.S.R. by 17 June, 1946, 3 o'clock P.M. Each person may take at most 30 kilos baggage. The place of assembly is the Friedland railway station, 3:30 P.M. Apartments and houses should be locked, keys surrendered to the police at the assembly point at the station, along with the corresponding signature of the owner.*
>
> *I draw your attention to the fact that any willful damage, destruction, etc. to the property or its contents shall be punished by death!*
>
> > *For the County Commission,*
> > *V. Kysela, e.H.*

*And here yet another Proclamation:*

> *It has been ordered that, effective immediately, all persons of German nationality age 6 years and up shall wear the following sign:*

*A white circle 15 centimeters in diameter upon which a 2 cm thick letter "N" of black linen is sewn, whose edge is 1 cm within the edge of the circle. This sign shall be worn on the left breast. Germans who were members of the NSDAP, the SA, the SS, NS Public Welfare office, NS Women's Association, NSKK, or any other division of the Party, must wear this sign on the back.*

*All Germans are forbidden to ride public transportation, visit public places of entertainment or parks!*

*All Germans are forbidden to leave their dwellings after 8 P.M.*

*If Russian or Czechoslovakian officers are met or chanced upon in the street or elsewhere, Germans must remove their hats or caps and pass by at an appropriate distance.*

*Store purchases are allowed one hour before closing. The badges must be procured by each German himself in accordance with the prescribed design. Non-compliance with the above mentioned order is punishable.*

*Any citizen of different nationality shall also be subject to punishment for aiding, abetting or helping Germans in any manner!*

*The Captain of the National Guard*
*Service in the City of Troppau*

## The Testimony of Albin Vorndran

Albin Vorndran, today a resident of Erlangen, was among those forced to wear the "N" badge. (N is the first letter in the Czech word for German, *Nemec*). In 1982 he gave the author the following statement.

*My name is Albin Vorndran and I was born on August 16, 1919. Because of a wound I received as a soldier in battle, I witnessed the entry of Russian troops into Roemerstadt, East Sudeten, as well as the expulsion of Germans from this city at the hands of the Czechs. Most men of my age were either in the war or prisoners of war and were therefore not witnesses to the expulsions. I was recovering from my wound while staying with my wife's parents, the Niesners, in Roemerstadt. They owned a bakery and a store that sold groceries and shoes.*

The Russians occupied Roemerstadt on May 4, 1945. A few days after their entry into town the Czech Svoboda Army came in and took over. All Czech soldiers were given three days' right to loot at will. They took anything they fancied. But that was just the start of the terror. An official proclamation was announced, whereby all Germans had to give up their radios and cameras. The death penalty threatened those who did not follow this order. As far as I know, all Germans surrendered their cameras. There was however one photographer in Roemerstadt who was allowed to keep his equipment; he had been ordered by the Russians to take passport and other photographs. But he was also threatened with death if he were to take photos of or for Germans. If the picture taken of me by this photographer at the end of May or beginning of June 1945 had been found on me during the expulsion, it would have gone badly for me. The "N" patch visible on the picture had to be worn by all Germans beginning in May 1945 until their expulsion.

In August 1945, the first Germans were driven out of their homeland like dogs. Individual family members were chosen at will and driven off to the railway station, where cattle cars stood ready. The cars had no roofs, and they were literally stuffed full of people. Old people as well as small children were forced into these cars, getting nothing to eat or drink. In these first days of expulsion the temperature averaged 30 degrees Centigrade [86 degrees Fahrenheit]. We were standing some 10 to 15 meters from these cattle cars but were not allowed to even once bring water or food to our relatives and friends. Even a priest, whose parents were part of the transport, was denied permission to bring something to his folks. He cried bitterly because he couldn't give his suffering parents so much as a drink of water. No one can imagine the pain and suffering that reigned over these families at such a sight, and as a consequence of these events. Probably because of protests from abroad these humiliating expulsions were stopped for a while. In any case, a second wave of expulsions began in January 1946. The regulations were that Germans could take only 50 kg of clothing and personal items, and 500 Reichsmarks with them. Whoever had more money than that had to give it up without restitution. My wife, her parents and I were expelled on March 1, 1946. First we were all assembled in a camp where our baggage was inspected, weighed and anything over 50 kg confiscated. Furthermore, things were taken from us which had been allowed by the regulations but which the Czechs *took a fancy to. There were incidents where people had their whole legal 50 kg taken away from them. After this first check we were body searched. First we had to leave our rooms so that they could be searched for any hidden jewelry or other objects left behind. Even the straw mattresses were emptied. Next we were taken one by one for the body search. I even had to take off my shoes for inspection, in the soles of which I had sewn 2,000 Reichsmarks. Luckily I had been wearing them this way for a few weeks and they were worn enough to escape detection. So I got through this part with little difficulty. Had they found the money, I would have been whipped, for it had been strictly forbidden to take more than 500 Reischsmark. On March 3, 1946, like the others before us, we were loaded onto cattle cars. The entire train was under heavy Czech military guard. As we headed off in the direction of Germany, no one knew what was to become of us.*

*Regarding confiscation of homes and businesses, I personally witnessed this as well. As already noted, my wife's parents owned a bakery and a store for groceries and shoes in Roemerstadt, Kirchenplatz 8. It was the last German business in the area. On the evening of October 21, 1945, around 6 P.M., a group of soldiers came in, locked us in a room, posted a guard at the door and kept us prisoner until 10 P.M. During that time two men ransacked the bakery, the other business and the apartment. Around 10 P.M. we had to go up to the second floor where we were again locked in. The next day we were taken to jail, where I was beaten. The reason for the beating was not that I had broken some law, it was because I was German. That was also the reason for our imprisonment. Moreover, as we discovered later, during the time we were in jail our home and business had been completely looted. Since they couldn't prove Party membership or any other transgressions on our part, we were released on the night of October 31 around 11 P.M. Fortunately we had a place to stay with some relatives, as we were not permitted to return to our own house. Thus, overnight, our property and possessions were gone.*

Pictures of Sudeten Germans wearing the "N" patch can be found in the German Archives, mementos of an era ruled by revenge and the *lex talionis*.

It seemed that not even the Czechs had learned from their pains and tribulations. They had fought against Hitler, but after the war they chose to follow his example, continue his inhuman methods.

Yet, this is only a part of the story. Some Germans were accorded proper and courteous treatment by the Czechs, whether on official business or at the workplace, creating a bright spot in an otherwise desperate situation. There were many instances of Czechs personally stepping in with a helping hand to assist the Sudenten Germans, easing their privations, especially in those areas where an enduring coexistence and a mutual respect had grown over many years, unaffected by any passing political constellation.

A special honor was earned by the relief action for German children organized by the Czech Premysl Pitter. The program was designed to care for children, abandoned and dying in camps, whose parents had died in the war or in postwar incidents, particularly in those Czech camps. At first there was some official opposition, but he nevertheless succeeded in bringing hundreds of children into the orphanages he built, and saved their lives.


## INTERNMENT CAMPS IN POLAND AND CZECHOSLOVAKIA

Not all Germans were driven from their homes in Poland and Czechoslovakia at the same time. However, the conditions grew steadily worse for those who remained. Thousands of them were interned in camps.

In Upper Silesia the former Nazi camp at Lamsdorf was turned into a camp for Germans designated for expulsion. Between August 1945 and the fall of 1946, 6,480 Germans perished here, among them 623 children.

During the 1970s the West German attorney general's office interrogated more than 100 people in an investigation of the Lamsdorf case. Names of camp officials accused of criminal acts were presented to the Polish courts. The Polish government and press disputed the charges, denying that any criminal acts had occurred. Due to a Polish amnesty law, prosecution was impossible. Furthermore, Poland regards the legal period of limitation as expired in such matters.

Lamsdorf was by no means the only camp where mass German fatalities took place. In a confidential report filed with the Foreign Office by R. W. F. Bashford, we read that

> the concentration camps were not dismantled, but rather taken over by the new owners. Mostly they are run by Polish militia. In Swientochlowice (Upper Silesia), prisoners who are not starved or whipped to death are made to stand, night after night, in cold water up to their necks, until they perish. In Breslau there are cellars from which, day and night, the screams of victims can be heard.[6]

A similar report dated August 28, 1945, submitted to the U.S. Senate, reads:

> In Y, Upper Silesia, an evacuation camp has been prepared which holds at present 1,000 people. . . . A great part of the people are suffering from symptoms of starvation; there are cases of tuberculosis and always new cases of typhoid. . . . Two people seriously ill with syphilis have been dealt with in a very simple way: They were shot. . . . Yesterday a woman from K was shot, and a child wounded.[7]

The International Committee of the Red Cross received similar reports. Since war's end it had tried to dispatch a standing delegation to Poland. Not until July 17, 1947, were Red Cross officials allowed to inspect an internment camp. Of course, by this time most Germans had been expelled or had died in the camps. Yet there were still a few camps where the Red Cross was not permitted to go.[8]

In Czechoslovakia, where the Red Cross had been let into a camp as early as the fall of 1945, the situation for Germans was not much better. Germans at the Svidnik camp, for example, were forced to clear away mine fields.[9]

Czech author Dr. H. G. Adler, a Jew who was imprisoned during the war in the Theresienstadt concentration camp, wrote about this installation, which had since been turned into an internment camp for Germans.

> Certainly there were those among them who, during the years of occupation, were guilty of some infraction or other, but the majority, among them children and adolescents, were locked up simply because they were German. Just because they were German . . . ? That phrase is frighteningly familiar; one could easily substitute the word "Jew" for "German." The rags given to the Germans as clothes were smeared with swastikas. They were miserably undernourished, abused, and generally subjected to much the same treatment one was used to in the German-run camps. . . . The camp was run by Czechs, yet they did nothing to stop the Russians from going in to rape the captive women. . . .[10]

## THE FATE OF THE DANUBE SWABIANS IN YUGOSLAVIA

The *Volksdeutsche,* the ethnic Germans who lived for centuries in southeastern Europe, were also swept away by war and expulsion. Their fates are less well known than those of the East Prussians, whose traumatic cataclysm is only now being discovered. A few extracts from eyewitness accounts are reproduced here, representative of the monstrous suffering this ethnic minority had to endure.

The Testimony of Roland Vetter

The Lutheran pastor Dr. Roland Vetter, who lost his parents in the maelstrom of the end of the war and expulsion, recalls:

> *In accordance with the will of the Reich government, the Germans were to be evacuated from the advancing front in the fall of 1944. At the end of September, the German population of the Banat streamed through Batschka in long columns of farm vehicles. On October 5th the Germans of Syrmia received the evacuation order; and on October 8th, Germans in Batschka got the same. Seventy per cent of the Danube Swabian population headed west, and not only in farm wagons, but on trains and even on canal boats.*
>
> *Conservative estimates placed 500,000 Swabians in Yugoslavia, 250,000 in Romania and 650,000 in Hungary. In Yugoslavia alone some 350,000 fled or were resettled (70.7% of the Germans there), 31,000 died fighting in the war (5.9%), and of the remainder, 55,000 (10.5%) died in the camps run by the subsequently empowered partisans. Approximately 30,000 survived. Today they represent a vanishing minority in the Yugoslavian State.*[11]

Characteristic of the attitude towards Germans in the country was the public sentencing of a high-placed cleric. On May 23, 1945, Dr. Philipp Popp, bishop of the German Evangelical Church in Yugoslavia, was arrested in Agram (Zagreb). He had previously refused to leave the country, and even now during the occupation he would not flee. After five weeks in prison, on June 28, 1945, the 2nd Partisan Army sentenced him to death by firing squad. The sentence was carried out the next day. His companion in misfortune, the Croatian Roman Catholic Archbishop Stepanic was sentenced to 16 years' imprisonment.

Regarding the occupation of former German communities by Soviet troops and Serbian partisans, Frau K.Z., born on December 20, 1903, resident in Neu-Werbas, gave this account after her deportation to Karlsruhe on April 16, 1947.

> *My hometown of Novi Vrbas was occupied by Serbian partisans and Soviet troops on October 19, 1944. . . . The partisans and soldiers went from house to house taking whatever they pleased. Homes were often broken into at night and women and girls were raped. The soldiers didn't care what age; for example, a fellow villager of my acquaintance, Frau Jakob Schneider née Beni, over*

*50, was raped along with her foster-daughter Iolanthe Hetzel née Schneider. Johanna Burbach, a 15-year-old girl whom I personally know quite well, was raped in front of her helpless parents. She later became pregnant and bore the child.*

Frau Katherina Hoffman gave this account of her time in the camp at Kecskemet in the summer of 1945:

*Whatever one could carry had to be dragged into the camp. The rest was brought in later by wagon. All money, gold and jewelry had already been taken away. . . . All women had their hair cut short, same with the children who had been segregated by sex. In the mornings we were given a soup made of flour and fat, sometimes made with petroleum jelly. There was no midday meal. In the evening a squash soup with a few noodles, a liter split among four people. We were awakened at 5 each morning. We had to work the whole day rebuilding the bombed-out train station; carrying the bricks and mortar, making walls, etc. People were often punished for going off to get food from private citizens.*

At the conclusion of the account she describes their expulsion:

*On the out-transport to Vienna we could take practically nothing. Some departed without shoes or socks, especially the children in the first transport. . . . Provisions were one kilogram of bread for four people, and the trip to Vienna took a week. Along the route potatoes and turnips were gathered up from fields and brought back to the rail cars during layovers. The last few clothes, bits of money or jewelry we had in those cars were taken from us. At the very end of our endurance we finally arrived in Vienna.*

Beyond the losses of life and limb there was the loss of one's property. The Danube Swabians in Yugoslavia were dispossessed of all property by law. While the goods and property of those who fled was being confiscated, the Germans who stayed behind had long been subject to a *de facto* separation from their house, farm, fields and/or business. At the beginning of 1945 vacated German houses were given to new settlers from the southern regions of the country (Montenegro, Bosnia). That sealed the dispossession for good.

The internment camps erected by the Tito government in Yugoslavia were hardly incidental to the sufferings that followed in the wake of Germany's retreat and eventual capitulation. Many thousands of Danube Swabians perished of starvation or abuse in the camps. Whole German or predominantly German villages and towns were sealed off with barbed wire, surrounded by armed guards; ethnic Germans resident there or rounded up from the surrounding regions were crowded by the dozens into houses and barns barren of furnishing or comfort, as all had been looted by the partisans. There was little or no food or medical care; internees were left to starve to death or perish from rampant disease. The purpose of these particular camps appears to have been to inflict misery and death on as many ethnic Germans as possible. The camps were decidedly not mere assembly points for group expulsion, they were consciously and officially recognized as extermination centers.

The place names of Rudolfsgnad, Gakovo, Jarek, Mitrovica, Molidorf and Kruschevlje, among others, remain burned into the memory of Danube Swabian survivors and their descendants. To this day, annual memorial services are held in places as far away as Philadelphia, Toronto and even Brazil, where survivors have found new homes as immigrants.[12]

## The Testimony of Justina Hoffmann

An additional account, among so many thousands of others from this sorrowful period, comes from Frau Justina Hoffmann, born October 20, 1906, in Sekic (county of Backa-Topola).

> *During the German downfall in the autumn of 1944 I was at home in Feketic with my husband Jakob Hoffmann and my 16-year-old son. We had a drapery and confectionery business there. Feketic had around 6,000 mostly Hungarian residents. There were about 2,000 Germans. On October 17, 1944, Russian troops marched into our town, followed a few days later by local partisans who took control. Our business was totally looted by the partisans in the first few days; everything had been hauled off.*
>
> *Women and girls had to hide themselves away every night in order to avoid being raped by Russian soldiers. One night I myself had to flee through a window. But even during the day women were not spared molestation by the soldiers. The wife of the master carpenter Andreas Koerper, a woman I knew, was raped in her home during the height of the day while a Russian soldier stood watch outside. In order to stifle her cries for help, a rag was stuffed in her mouth. Frau Elisabeth Weissmann née Glock, nearly 60 years old, was surprised in her home then raped by a drunken*

Russian soldier. Frau Sofia Dietrich, who refused to betray her daughter's hiding place, was so terribly beaten she was permanently disfigured.

All Germans were obliged to work the fields. On the night of November 17, 1944, most German men without regard to age were hauled out of their homes and severely maltreated. They were so badly beaten that blood flowed from numerous wounds, the mouth and nose. They were locked up in the town hall, my husband being one of them. Three days later all Germans, including myself and my son, were forcibly gathered together along with the 48 men who had been locked up, and force-marched to Backa-Topola. Once there the women were sent back to Feketic. We had to continue with work in the fields and were allowed to stay in our homes, even though they were still being broken into and looted, day and night, by Russian soldiers and partisans.

On January 16, 1945, we were thrown out of our homes once and for all and brought to the camp at Sekic. There were about 6,000 Germans from northern Batschka interned here. On January 27, 1945, I was transferred to the civilian internment camp, a starch factory, in Subotica. The Germans were packed into this place by the thousands. One hundred and seven women slept in the room where I was. Each day we had to assemble at 4:30 A.M., double rows standing for hours in the cold on the assembly ground. Partisans took us to our workplaces and brought us back at night. Each night we were counted off rank and file. When the numbers did not tally, which happened just about every other day, we had to remain standing in the cold often until midnight. Men and even women were badly mistreated. The men were often quartered in the room above ours, packed in so tightly they had to stand the whole night.

On May 24, 1945, I came back with about 400 other men and women to the Sekic camp. When their mothers were off working, the children were housed separately here. The kids were beaten whenever they tried to get to their mothers. These drawn, helpless children behind barbed wire were a horrible sight to behold. On October 1, 1945, the whole camp had to assemble, more than 8,000 people. Mothers with small children, the sick and invalid, old people and cripples, all of us were shipped off to the extermination camps at Gakovo, Krusevlje and Ridjica, where several thousands starved to death. Since I was still among the

*able-bodied, about 1,500 of us, they kept me back at Sekic. On
January 27, 1946, I decided to escape. My son had already been
dead since September among several other 14- to 16-year-old
boys. My husband had been deported.*

In closing it should be mentioned that parallel to the internments, large-scale executions of German men had begun, most mass liquidations. In Startschowa, for example, after a random selection during the night of October 22, 1944, 80 men were shot. Similar events occurred in Sartscha, Deutsch-Zerne and many other communities in the Banat as well as Batschka. A group of partisans shot Germans in Hodschag; a liquidation commando rounded up about 350 men in Filipovo on October 25, shooting 240 of them. It is not unrealistic to assume that there were regular execution units among the partisans who went from one Danube Swabian town to another fulfilling their special task.[13]

We hear so much today about the so-called ethnic cleansing going on since 1991 in the former Yugoslavia. Forty-eight years ago another genocide was in progress in the same areas of the Balkans. Hundreds of thousands of ethnic Germans were uprooted, and tens of thousands were killed. They were evicted from their homes and sent off to slave labor camps in the Soviet Union; the women were raped and old people and children too young to work were interned in starvation camps.

Many of the survivors of that ethnic cleansing eventually came to the United States and became American citizens. Some of them may actually be our neighbors, and yet who has cared to listen to their stories? Most of them, not expecting any sympathy or understanding, have kept quiet for decades. Today they are starting to talk.

## The Testimony of Elisabeth Walter

One such survivor is Mrs. Elisabeth Walter, who lives today in Barrington, Illinois, a German-American who came to the United States in 1950 at the age of 9. She was born in Karlsdorf (now Banatski Karlovac), in the agricultural region known as the Banat, today part of the Voivodina, in the former Yugoslavia.

I interviewed her on January 8, 1993:

*Before World War I the Banat belonged to Hungary. After the
war it was divided into three parts, which were allocated to
Hungary, Romania and Yugoslavia. Karlsdorf was settled by
German pioneers around 1800, and there were about half a
million ethnic Germans living in similar towns throughout the*

former Yugoslavia. Our ancestors came from Germany to settle the then empty lands when Empress Maria Theresia reigned Austria-Hungary. The settlers were given land that was wilderness, which they in turn cultivated and were allowed to homestead. We had kept our German language, heritage and traditions all those years.

What I remember about my early years is mostly war: sirens, bombing, soldiers and fear. In the fall of 1944 and early spring of 1945 my father, as well as all other ethnic German men aged fifteen to fifty, and all women ages sixteen to thirty, had been sent off to labor camps. I recall watching from our bedroom window soldiers beating children with the butts of their guns as they ran along the wagons that were taking their mothers away. Thousands upon thousands were shipped off to Russia in cattle cars to work in the coal mines as slave laborers.

One night in April 1945 soldiers burst into our home awakening my family. They grabbed my mother and tore her wedding ring and earrings off. With nothing but the clothes on our backs and a few small bundles under my mother's and grandmother's arms we were driven into the dark. I was petrified as I clung to my grandmother and we joined the large crowd in the middle of the street. The whole town was taken in this manner and herded out of Karlsdorf to the airport just outside the town. We were put into the hangars, which were surrounded by a high barbed wire fence. We slept on the bare, cold and damp dirt floor. No heat was provided, so that the condensation from the people breathing would rise to the ceiling and in the morning, as it cooled off, it would drip down on us like rain.

Throughout Yugoslavia all ethnic Germans were put into concentration camps and became prisoners of the state. We lost our citizenship and all our property was confiscated. I, too, at the tender age of four, was considered a political prisoner and a threat to the security of Yugoslavia. From 1945 to 1949 we suffered starvation, beatings, mass murders and slave labor. People from other towns were brought to our camp. In all some 4,000 human beings were packed into the two airplane hangers. Hunger, fear and sickness were our way of life. Every morning the able-bodied adults had to assemble outside the hangar, stand at attention and listen to the morning propaganda. Then all had to shout "Schivio Tito!" (Long live Tito!) before being marched off to work. Older *children were also gathered up and put to work in the fields or to carry wood for the camp from fifteen miles away. I stayed behind with the younger children. I remember looking out of the fence and wishing to be on the other side; there was a field of poppies bloming and I wanted more than anything to run through them and pick an armful. I waited daily at the gate for my mother to return, hoping that she would bring back additional food, which she would hide in her underclothing. Food had to be concealed from the eyes of the guards, because if you were caught you had to pay dearly.*

*Time has no season in my memory. I can remember some things as if they were yesterday, and others as in a dream. I must have been five or six by the time we were no longer in the hangar but in a blocked-off section of town. Soldiers were stationed at the end of the streets. We were in houses with fifteen or more people in each room, where we slept on the straw-covered floor. I remember crying as my grandparents were being taken away. All old people and children with no mothers were being taken away. Many years later we learned that they had been taken to Rudolfsgnad, which was a death camp. Two of my grandparents died there of starvation. One survived.*

*Lice were also a fact of life. Everyone had them because there was no soap. Some days we were given pea soup. The peas were infested with bugs that crunched as you bit into them. Malnutrition took its toll. Sickness was all around. Open sores were very common. I remember I had boils on my abdomen that did not heal for a long time; they always oozed with pus. Typhoid and other illnesses were rampant. There were no doctors or medication. Thus people died daily. Soon wagonloads of bodies were carted off to mass graves and tossed in. My cousin died of typhoid. My brother also came down with it. He was very sick and came close to death, but somehow he recovered without medicine. Only the very strong could survive those conditions.*

*By the fall of 1947 we had been in three or four different camps. In September of that year we came to Gakova, a camp not far from the Hungarian border. One night my mother, brother, myself, my aunt, two cousins and some other women sneaked out of the camp. All had pooled their scarce possessions and paid a guide. I remember walking aimlessly through the cornfields at night. Suddenly someone called out: "He's gone. We're lost!" Our guide had deserted us. One of the women claimed she could orient herself by the stars, and so we followed her all night and in the morning we found ourselves back where we had started: Gakova. The guards found us and we were locked up in a windowless room with 50 or so other prisoners, in total darkness with no room to sit or lie down to sleep or rest.*

*When we were released from there my mother and aunt once more managed to scrape some dinars together, and this time we did escape, walking across the Hungarian countryside for more than a month. We hid and slept in the cornfields and walked through the rainy fall weather. For days we did not see the sun. We came to a large empty field. Someone took me by the hand and we ran as fast as we could across the flat, empty range, my feet hardly touching the ground. Shots rang out. We were being fired at! This must have been the border between Hungary and Austria. . . .*

## The Testimony of Anna Tiesler

Another survivor of the internment and starvation is Anna Tiesler, who now lives in Philadelphia. I interviewed her on January 8, 1993:

*Our ancestors migrated from Germany to the Batschka around 1776 in search of a better future. I was born in Prigrevica Sv. Ivan in 1929, the oldest of three children. My father was the manager of the local brick factory. Life was peaceful within the family and with our neighbors, the Serbs, the Croats and the Hungarians. We were brought up Catholic and learned Serbo-Croat in school. All this tranquility ended in 1941 when our country was overrun by Hitler. War came and with it a lot of pain. All our young—and not so young—men were conscripted into the German army. Luckily my father was able to stay home at first—partly because of a heart condition, and partly because of his responsibility for the brick factory, which suddenly was considered of vital importance in the war effort. Then, one day in 1944 he, too, was drafted and became another of the thousands of Volksdeutsche missing in action.*

*In October 1944 the Soviet troops came and life became very hard. With no men to protect us, the Russian soldiers had sport with the women of the town. Every night, after partying, they stalked the town and systematically raped young and old. Some-time in December 1944 the women aged 17 to 32 were sent to Russia to work in the coal mines. My mother was past that age, but still they sent her to dig trenches between the fronts. As I was fifteen years old it was a big responsibility for me to take care of my younger brother and sister as well as the livestock.*

*When the Soviet troops left, Marshall Tito's partisans took over. That is when the final curtain came down on us. During the night of March 15, 1945, there was a knock on the door and we were told to be out of the house in two hours, take one change of clothing and leave everything else behind. Doors and closets had to remain unlocked. We were driven out of the town, and after an exhausting two-day march we were consigned to an internment camp. Many old people, who could not endure the forced marching, were shot or beaten to death. Others were left dying along the road. My Hungarian-born grandmother was with us.*

*As we arrived in Filipovo, another German-speaking town, we were herded in as cattle into any space available. After one week, we were driven to a large field and separated. My sister, Eva, was too young to work and was selected out to one side. My brother, Josef, at the time twelve years old, was considered a man, and was taken away from me. My sister and grandmother, with all the too young and too old for work, were put in cattle trains with no sanitary facilities and sent off to a dreadful concentration camp by the name of Gakovo, near the Hungarian border.*

*In the meantime, my mother had come back from digging trenches and had landed in a camp in Sombor, where she found out that the inhabitants of our town had been expelled from their homes and interned in camps. Determined to find her children, she escaped from Sombor and made her way to Filipovo, where she found me. We were then assigned to a labor camp and worked in the fields from six in the morning to dark, seven days a week. Our quarters consisted of completely empty rooms with a little straw on the floor and as many people in one room as would fit. Before bedtime, we had to check the straw for snakes—some of them poisonous—prevalent in the area. Lice and mice were an awful plague. Food consisted of soup broth with a slice of cornbread in the morning and a cup of bean soup in the evening. While there I contracted pneumonia and malaria. I was not treated, since there was no doctor in the camp—or any medicine.*

*All my mother had was a small sheet, which she wet and wrapped me in over and over until my fever broke. It was a slow recovery.*

*My mother was, of course, very worried about her two other children. She kept telling me, "I must find them." Thus, by the fall of 1945, my strength was a little better and we escaped to look for them, not having any idea where they might be. We could only walk by night and through the fields. We walked several nights until we arrived in our hometown, where we heard that my brother and sister were in Gakovo. After two trying days of walking, we arrived at the camp, and found them among the 21,000 inmates. We were overjoyed to see them, and horrified by their condition. My sister had no skin left on her legs and my brother was not much better. The death rate was very high—between 50 and 55 per day. The unlucky ones were buried in mass graves near the camp. I, too, have family members in those mass graves.*

*With the help of a Macedonian worker at the old brick factory—who in the meantime had become the "big boss"—we were able to escape from Gakovo. My sister could hardly walk for the blood ran down her sore legs, but we had to go on. We hid at the brick factory and received help from our Hungarian friends, who left food in certain places for us. In the spring of 1946 we were found out and taken back to Gakovo.*

*One more winter under those conditions would have meant our death. Thus, in the fall of 1946 we again planned our escape, this time to Hungary. At the border some unlucky person was captured, and while he was taken away, we managed to cross over. Language was no problem, since my mother and I both spoke Hungarian. For two weeks we walked through Hungary, begging for food and sleeping in barns. Finally, we crossed the border into Austria, where we lived in a refugee camp at Eisenerz until 1954, when our whole family immigrated to America.*

## The Testimony of Eva Edl

Mrs. Tiesler's younger sister, Eva Edl, lives today in Aiken, South Carolina. In an interview on January 9, 1993, she confirmed her sister's account and added:

*Our town was established in the 18th century by settlers from various parts of Germany and Austria. The towns and villages in this area were German, Hungarian, Serbian or Croatian, with*

*distinctive costumes, language and traditions, but our relation-
ship was friendly.*

*In March 1941 Germany invaded Yugoslavia and German
planes annihilated a contingent of the Yugoslavian army near our
home just outside the town. My father found one survivor, clothed
him in his own civilian clothes, and helped him to escape. He also
made an effort to help members of other ethnic groups during the
German occupation, a fact that some of them remembered when
our family was in dire need in 1945 and 1946.*

*After the Red Army came, many men and women were shipped
off to slave-labor camps in the Soviet Union. Others were re-
cruited for local labor. In March 1945 we were evicted from our
homes and forced to march to Filipovo. I heard shots, cries, reports
of people being killed and women giving birth on the roadside.
My grandmother and I, who could not work, were locked into
cattle cars for approximately two days without food, water or
toilet facilities and transported to the internment camp at
Gakovo. Our diet there consisted of one ladleful of soup in the
morning and again at night. The soup was nothing but warm,
saltless water containing a few peas; the only solid food we
received was a small piece of dried cornmeal mush distributed
once or twice a week. Soon there were outbreaks of diarrhea,
dysentery and other diseases. However, no medical treatment
whatever was available, and people started dying all around me.
The dead were thrown into the mass graves, which were then
covered over, leaving no trace of the identity of the victims. I
myself had developed large festering sores all over my body, with
hardly any skin left on my thighs and hips.*

Yet another American of Danube Suevian origin is Anna Selgrad, née Reith,
who immigrated to the United States in the 1950s and lives today in Crystal
River, Florida. She was born in 1934 in Tscheb (also known as Cib, and today
as Celarevo) in the Batschka. Her ancestors from the Black Forest, in what is
today the province of Baden-Württemberg in Germany, settled in Tscheb in
the 18th century and were already mentioned in the registry in 1802.

On 10 January 1993 she gave me this account:

*When the Soviet front came closer in October 1944 the people
from our village started to trek West in covered wagons. Since our
family was just common laborers and my father was a carpenter,*

*we did not own any wagons and thus we were not able to leave. My father, who was still in civilian clothes when the Soviet Army came, was detained and we never heard from him again.*

*In November 1944 the Soviets took away all the men from age 14 to 50. Most of them were killed. Also in November women aged 16 to 40 were deported. My mother got herself ready and even said goodbye to us, but they went past our house without taking her along, probably because of my little brother, who was not even two years old at the time. In December they took the rest of the men from 50 years up and the women aged 40 to 50. From December 1944 to June 1945 our lives were in the hands of the partisans, and we had to do whatever they wanted. Early in the morning of June 2, 1945 they started on one end of the town taking everyone from their homes and we were all driven together like cattle to a factory by the town. There family after family was searched over, extra clothes were taken away, as well as pillows, blankets and all our jewelry; earrings were ripped off, without opening them. We were taken to two houses, under heavy guard, given some straw to sleep on, and kept there for three weeks, with very little food. On June 23 we all had to stand in line, the children in front, the grownups in back. My sister, who was 12 years old, and I, who was 11, stood with our brother between us, but someone told us to take him back to our mother, who was standing in line with her mother, aged 76. As we started to walk, my sister was taken away from me and had to stay behind, as well as my cousin, aged 11; my aunt with two younger children and my father's mother were taken with the rest of us, including the mother of our neighbor here in Florida, Mathias Kreitschitz—in all some 105 persons. We walked some nine miles to the next town, where we were put in open cattle wagons and taken to the starvation camp in Jareck, Batschka. There were some 25,000 or more starving children and old people in this camp.*

*For food we had dried bean straw, cooked in water with all the bugs and filth, and feed corn, twice a day. There were no cats or dogs or birds—of course, whatever could be caught was eaten. Every morning at sunrise everyone who was able to walk had to go outside, and then just march in the fields. Many never came back; those who could not keep up were left behind and often shot. After we were there for two weeks, they sent the younger women to work in another camp, including my mother, leaving me with my maternal grandmother and my brother, who was getting weaker by the day. He died of starvation on July 26, 1945. Friends and relatives were dying daily, some too weak to move and rats all over them. When my mother finally came back to us, the shock that her son was dead nearly killed her, yet she had to worry about me because I became sick with malaria. On September 16 my mother's mother died, and all this time we had no news about my sister.*

*On April 3, 1946, the camp, which now had only about 2,800 people left, was moved to Krushivel, near the Hungarian border. My sister, who had escaped from her camp, showed up in September 1946. There were seven of us left, but in February 1947 my paternal grandmother died. Before that, however, on January 7, 1947, a man helped us to escape to Hungary, walking about 22 miles in two feet of snow and bitter cold from 6 P.M. until 3 A.M. It then took us one week to walk through Hungary and we had many scares on the way. But on January 14, 1947, we were free in Austria, only to be captured and put in a displaced persons camp in Trofaiach, Styria. Thank God we found there food (not too much) and a bed, and we were safe. In February 1950 I married, and our daughter and son were born at the D.P. camp in Judenburg, Styria. On July 10, 1955 we were able to immigrate to the United States and came to Milwaukee. It was very hard for us at first, because we did not speak English. My husband Karl started working for an envelope factory, and I was able to learn a trade in 1964—tool and die. Meanwhile, in December 1960 we became American citizens. We were finally not just a number.*

*My husband's family went through the same ordeal, in the Banat, also in the former Yugoslavia. His family was also deported to a starvation camp. My sister and her family also migrated to the United States, as well as my husband's sister with her family. Our two children are married and we have six grandchildren.*

Life goes on. Is there better proof of it than this? But who knows anything about these events? Hitherto it would seem that the blackout on this period of history has been complete. Half a million people were simply wiped off Yugoslavia's history. As Elisabeth Walter observed, "It is hard when you lose everything you own, but unbearable when you lose your identity and history."

## ANGLO-AMERICAN VOICES AGAINST THE EXPULSIONS

"If the conscience of men ever again becomes sensitive, these expulsions will be remembered to the undying shame of all who committed or connived at them. . . . The Germans were expelled, not just with an absence of over-nice consideration, but with the very maximum of brutality."[14]

This is how British publisher and author Victor Gollancz judged the expulsions of the Germans in his remarkable book *Our Threatened Values,* published in 1946. Gollancz was a socialist and a Jew; he was a tireless champion for human rights and human dignity everywhere. Before the war he published a series of books against Hitler, including one by exiled Czech Minister Hubert Ripka.

Other than Gollancz's, there were few voices of protest heard. Among them was the noted philosopher Bertrand Russell who wrote in *The Times* for October 19, 1945:

> In eastern Europe now mass deportations are being carried out by our allies on an unprecedented scale, and an apparently deliberate attempt is being made to exterminate many millions of Germans, not by gas, but by depriving them of their homes and of food, leaving them to die by slow and agonizing starvation. This is not done as an act of war, but as a part of a deliberate policy of "peace." . . . It was decreed by the Potsdam agreement that expulsions of Germans should be carried out "in a humane and orderly manner." And it is well known, both through published accounts and through letters received in the numerous British families which have relatives or friends in the armies of occupation, that this proviso has not been observed by our Russian and Polish allies. It is right that expression should be given to the immense public indignation that has resulted, and that our allies should know that British friendship may well be completely alienated by the continuation of this policy.[15]

The Relief Commission of the International Committee of the Red Cross reported:

> On 27 July 1945, a boat arrived at the West Port of Berlin which contained a tragic cargo of nearly 300 children, half dead from hunger, who had come from a "home" at Finkenwalde in Pomerania. Children from two to fourteen years old lay in the

bottom of the boat, motionless, their faces drawn with hunger, suffering from the itch and eaten up by vermin. Their bodies, knees and feet were swollen—a well-known symptom of starvation.[16]

This same picture of starving children, mostly orphans, was repeated time and again in the months and years following the war. *Time* magazine took up the subject, and published in its issue for November 12, 1945, a picture of three orphans from Danzig. Under the heading "Sins of the Fathers" the commentary read:

These three German children are paying for the sins their fathers may have committed. They are "displaced" orphans, turned out of a Polish orphanage in Danzig and sent back to Germany in tightly packed cattle trucks, without medical care and almost without food. The Poles, many of whose children looked like these not long ago, are clearing all hospitals of German patients, no matter how sick. The boy at the left is nine years old, weighs 40 lbs., is too weak to stand. The boy in the center is twelve, weighs 46 lbs. His sister (right) is eight, weighs 37 lbs. They are being cared for by a British nurse in Berlin's British zone.

The Berlin correspondent for the London *Times* filed this similar report on September 10, 1945:

In the Robert Koch Hospital here, which I visited this morning, there are more than sixty German women and children, many of whom were summarily evicted from a hospital and an orphanage in Danzig last month, and, without food and water or even straw to lie on, were dispatched in cattle trucks to Germany. When the train arrived in Berlin they said that of eighty-three persons crammed into two of the trucks twenty were dead.

A woman recovering from typhoid had, she stated, seen her husband beaten to death by Poles and she had then been driven from her farm near Danzig to work in the fields. Now she has survived the journey to Berlin with two young sons, and, without money, clothes or relations, cannot see what the future holds.

Three orphans I saw aged between eight and twelve are still almost skeletons after ten days' treatment, owing to the almost complete lack of fats in Berlin; none of them weighed more than three stone.

Another small boy turned out of Danzig had a scrawled postcard attached to him stating that his soldier father was long since missing and that his mother and two sisters had died of hunger.[17]

On October 18, General Dwight D. Eisenhower telegraphed Washington:

> In Silesia, Polish administration and methods are causing a mass exodus westward of German inhabitants. Germans are being ordered out of their homes and to evacuate New Poland. Many unable to move are placed in camps on meager rations and under poor sanitary conditions. Death and disease rate in camps extremely high. . . . Methods used by Poles definitely do not conform to Potsdam agreement. . . .
>
> Breslau death rate increased tenfold and death rate reported to be 75% of all births. Typhoid, typhus, dysentery, and diphtheria are spreading.
>
> Total number potentially involved in westward movement to Russian zone of Germany from Poland and Czechoslovakia in range of 10 million. . . . No coordinated measures yet taken to direct stream of refugees into specific regions or provide food and shelter. . . . [There exists] serious danger of epidemic of such great proportion as to menace all Europe, including our troops, and to probability of mass starvation [on an] unprecedented scale.[18]

These warnings caused the Allies to lodge protests through their embassies in Warsaw and Prague. They at least achieved a reduction of expulsions into the American and British zones of occupation.

## "ORDERLY" RESETTLEMENT

Although the process of expelling millions of Germans from Eastern Europe cannot be termed orderly or humane, the deportations were not entirely chaotic. There was a phase of "orderly" resettlement, arranged between the Allies and the countries demanding expulsion of their German populations.

The Potsdam Protocol did not, however, speak only of an "orderly" resettlement but rather of a "humane" one. Yet how can forced resettlement, being uprooted from one's ancestral homeland, ever be considered "humane"? Is not involuntary resettlement by its very nature *in*humane? The psychological ravages that uprooting causes makes physical pain pale by comparison. The Allies ignored this fact, and chose to throw a mantle of legality—and hypocrisy—over the much greater infamy of the uprooting: It should not be perceived as what it was, a brutal expulsion, it should be justified as a so-called orderly transfer.

For that reason the Western Allies at first sought to impose a moratorium on expulsions at Potsdam. When it was not observed, they tried to get a hold on the expulsions through the machinery of the Control Council in Berlin, to steer them into a predictable schedule, established on November 20, 1945.

The first expulsions following the new plan for "orderly" resettlement were conducted in Czechoslovakia, Poland and Hungary in January 1946. Compliance with the new regulations was still unsatisfactory. This was how General Lucius Clay described it:

> The first trainload from Hungary was a pitiful sight. The expellees had been assembled without a full allowance of food and personal baggage, and arrived hungry and destitute. As a result of representations repeated many times, arrangements were made to permit a small baggage allowance and to provide each expellee with RM 500. Difficulties were likewise experienced with the Czechs, not only in the withholding of personal possessions but also in withholding young, able workers while sending to us the aged, the women, and small children. Only after halting the movement temporarily could we remedy these conditions by negotiations.[19]

One example typical of many later resettlements is the "de-Germanization" of Deutschbohl (today Boly), a Hungarian village in the Danube-Drava triangle, 200 km south of Budapest.

## The Testimony of Franz Tischler

Franz Tischler, a Suevian from Hungary and resident of Germany since the 1950s, remembers:

> *The Hungarian population was somewhat reserved with regard to the group designated for expulsion, but by no means hostile. The Catholic Church remained quite passive in the face of these events, offering no help to its members in need.*
>
> *The expulsion began toward the end of June 1946 and affected about one-third of the village's population. Each person was allowed*

*one suitcase which was inspected by the police. The expulsion was by train, in freight cars, and it can be described as orderly. It took four days. Provisions during the trip were adequate in consideration of prevailing conditions. The destination for the expellee train from Deutshbohl was Bad Schwalbach near Wiesbaden.*

*The citizens of Bad Schwalbach and vicinity were very withdrawn toward the newcomers, something quite understandable for people who were hungry, cold and living in catastrophic circumstances in a bombed out city.*[20]

## TRAINS FROM CZECHOSLOVAKIA

Whereas there are relatively few photographs or films that show the brutality of the expulsions in the summer and fall of 1945, later "organized transfers" in 1946 and 1947 were recorded for posterity.

One such film was made in the summer of 1946 by the American Army, designed to capture an exemplary resettlement. Whoever sees it today gets an impression that resettlements could be orderly, after all. In it we see American officers and Czech officials discussing the resettlement; Sudeten German women and children—here were very few men—carrying their baggage to the trains; they are not being beaten or mistreated, which, according to countless reports, was often the case when no camera was around.

They board the trains. Most are standing, but the trains are nonetheless not quite as full as they were in 1945 or early 1946. Then the frontier is crossed, into the American zone of Germany. The passengers throw away their "expellee" armbands: hundreds of armbands, flying out of windows and doors, for in Bavaria they will need no armbands.[21]

The arrival in Bavaria was not always happy, however. How many had left relatives behind in the Sudetenland, interned or otherwise not permitted to leave because their professional expertise was needed for the time being? Moreover, the refugee quarters were cramped and dilapidated. It was not like home before the war.

Here is a German family resigned to its fate. Frau Anna Matzka sits, mute; she does not cry anymore. She is 82. (See photo p. xl)

For the most part the children do not understand what is going on around them. They just know they are hungry. Everywhere the same scenes of misery. Here an orphan with an empty stare; there a boy searching out something edible in a garbage can.

A documentary film entitled *Daybreak* was made under the auspices of the World Church Service by the New York Film Society International Film Foundation in 1947-48. Among other things it shows numerous camps for expelled ethnic Germans and "displaced persons" in Austria, primarily in and around Linz, the Salzkammergut and Salzburg. Framed in this context, the film describes the postwar experiences of the Danube Swabians through the story of a repatriated German from Yugoslavia, Dr. Roland Vetter (see pp. 95-96).[22]

## ABDUCTED INTO THE SOVIET UNION

As previously mentioned, the Yalta Conference granted war reparations to the Soviet Union in the form of labor services. According to German Red Cross documents, it is estimated that 874,000 German civilians were abducted to the Soviet Union. Of these so-called reparations deportees, 45% perished.

The Danube Swabians and Siebenbuerger Saxons were hardest hit, not to mention in particular the East Prussians and Pomeranians. Their fates, unrecorded on film or photographs, are described in the following personal accounts.

### The Testimony of a Man from Siebenbuergen, Romania

*I was a noncommissioned officer in the Romanian army reserves when, on January 27, 1945, a detachment of the Soviet military came to my unit and rounded up all the Germans in it—I am a German from Siebenbuergen, and at that time I was a Romanian citizen, 27 years old. Eleven of us Germans in Romanian uniform were brought to Diemrich/Deva in Siebenbuergen. There we were loaded onto freight trains arriving from the Banat, already filled with abducted Germans. We were headed east. I was unable to let either my family or friends know. I found out later that my wife had already been arrested in the southern Siebenbuergen city of Schaessburg on January 15, and deported to the USSR. Our 11 year old son had to be left behind with my mother-in-law.*

*After about a month and a half the train arrived in Ufaley with its cargo of some 1,500 people, a huge nickel mine between Tcheliabinsk and Svetlovsk. We were housed in three massive barracks, and only a short time after arrival typhoid fever broke out, killing 350 to 400 people. In spite of this we were forced to work, all of us, German men and women from Romania. We had to work underground mining nickel. Since food was lacking as much as safety measures in the mines, accidental death accompanied the deaths from fever. Sometimes I worked in the open pit mine. We also cut trees for the plank roads upon which the automatic dump trucks traveled, modern equipment delivered to the Soviet Union by the USA. The work was brutal. The law stipulating that work cannot be performed if the temperature is too low was never enforced. Mine cave-ins, felling trees in subzero temperatures, fainting spells for lack of food, all led to fatal consequences, an unending chain. Day in, day out, all we got to eat was cabbage leaf soup, sometimes with kasha, a barley porridge. In order to offset the hunger pangs we had to drink a lot of water, which resulted in bloating—pressing a finger on one's thigh left a depression. We got very little money for our work; most of our pay was withheld by the administration office. If someone did not meet his work quota, all money was withheld, which also could have fatal results, for in such cases extra food could not be purchased.*

*Due to the infestation of bedbugs and other vermin there were always waves of spotted fever breaking out. We were also afflicted with a type of malaria, called "Volhynian fever" in these parts. Because of this the administration was often organizing medical transports which would take the sick back home if they could no longer work. But the administration also played jokes on us. Once, in the spring of 1948, we were told that the best, most productive workers would be able to go home. I was among them. They came to get us at night, putting us into trucks . . . but not to go home, to ship out via Tcheliabinsk to Nias instead, to work in the SIS Truck Factory along with 5,000 German prisoners of war, even though we were not POWs but civilian deportees.*

*We had no letters from home. Even though we were given postcards from the camp administration on which we could write a few words and return to the office to be sent out for us, there was never any word from our families. Shortly before the camp was disbanded we found the answer to this riddle. Our postcards had been thrown into the trash, never sent at all. It was years later when I found out that my wife, just like most other German women and men from Siebenbuergen, had been deported to the Ukraine, in the region around Stalino, Konstantinovska, Enakyevo and Petrovska. My wife, by profession a bookkeeper, as*

*well as I, a teacher, withstood these years with relatively little
damage to our health since we were both athletic and still young
enough to endure.*

*On June 28, 1948, in Nias, we were chased out of our cots
shortly after midnight, as was always the case in such instances,
separated into groups according to our home origin in
Siebenbuergen, and loaded onto freight trains. Approximately one
month later I was back home. I had to wait another whole year
before my wife returned. During the whole time we were apart I
was unable to learn anything of her fate.*[23]

Another survivor of the deportations to the Soviet Union was Josef Weber
of the Banat, Romania, today a resident of Kitchener, Ontario, Canada. He was
interviewed by Hans Bergel, a writer originally from Siebenbuergen, who
collected this and similar moving accounts for a radio program broadcast in
Germany in 1985, entitled "As the Exodus Began—The Trials of the Germans
in Siebenbürgen and the Banat."

### The Testimony of Josef Weber

*Our transport took us to the region between Sverdlovsk in the
north and Tcheliabinsk in the south, east of the Urals. Our trip
had taken 42 days. Due to illness and the lack of any medical
attention our once huge group had been decimated, not only
during transport but also after our arrival, when we were forced
to live for two weeks under the open sky, exposed to the 30-degree
cold. I worked outdoors in one of the many camps near Ufaley.
Shortly before I was transferred to Nyassepetrovsk I finally heard
something about my wife, who was then 21 years old. I met an
acquaintance who told me that she had also been deported, and
that he had met her in a mine near Stalino.*

*In the winter of 1949-50 I injured my right leg while clearing
trees. It was so bad that after suffering weeks of festering and
wound fever, the Soviet camp administration put me down for
the next westbound medical transport. Three weeks before this I
was told that my wife, at the work camp in the Ukraine, had died
of silicosis, or dust-lung. After I had traveled for weeks via Kiev
to first Frankfurt-on-the-Oder, finally Berlin, all I wanted was
to go back home to my Banat. For two years I suffered in hospitals,*

*going from doctor to doctor. When I was finally cured in 1952, I got the news that the Romanian authorities had evacuated the German inhabitants of my hometown near the Romanian-Yugoslavian border, along with 50,000 other Germans. They were set out on the Danubian Steppes at the beginning of winter, under the open sky, no roofs over their heads! My elderly parents died there within two weeks. Thus, none of my family were left in my former homeland, for even my three-year-old son was dead of an undetermined illness one month after my wife had been deported in February 1945; an older brother was killed at the front near Stalingrad in 1942; and my sister died in 1949 as a deportee in the Soviet Union.*

## The Testimony of a Woman from Siebenbuergen

*On January 15, 1945, together with thousands of others, I was plucked out of my home in a central Siebenbuergen city. A uniformed Romanian policeman and a Soviet soldier forced their way into our house. They gave me just enough time to pack a small suitcase and then escorted me out. Armed men in uniform were hauling people out of just about every other house, too. We were interned in a school building. I was 18 years old.*

*One week later we were packed into cattle cars fitted with double-deck wooden cots and taken to Rimnicul-Sarat on the Moldau River, east of the eastern Carpathians. There we were transferred to broad-gauge railway cattle cars of the Soviet line. These were also outfitted with wood-plank cots, plus a tiny iron stove, and a hole sawed into the wood floor as a toilet for both men and women. There were about 1,000 of us in the entire train. During the 32 days of our journey via Odessa, Kiev, Krivoi Rog to Kungur in the Urals, we were allowed to leave the train twice, both times at night. We were given a warm meal three times, the rest of the time we had to make do with the small rations we had brought from home. People between 16 and 55 years old were among us.*

*In Kungur we were unloaded in 40-degree cold, then taken to a church which became our home for about three months. Some of the men were taken to build wooden barracks where we were later supposed to live. But after a few days spotted fever broke out*

*in the church due to the masses of vermin we had acquired . . .*
*139 of us died. Food consisted of one meal of chick peas per day,*
*300 grams of bread and a finger-sized piece of fish or meat. We*
*were taken out to work before the barracks were finished. We*
*women had to work outside in the freezing cold with crowbars,*
*cramp irons and shovels to load cast-iron blocks the size of fruit*
*crates into trucks; the blocks were along the railroad siding and*
*we had to break them free of the ice that covered them. They were*
*then hauled to the blast furnaces. This was essentially our work*
*for the next five years. The first two were the hardest. Our lack*
*of nourishment led to all sorts of illnesses; and due to the 12-hour*
*work days and a complete lack of sanitation, deaths were frequent.*
*I saw women who had so exerted themselves their uterus protruded*
*from the vagina; others who, due to the lack of protein in the*
*years' long diet of cabbage soup, developed open, festering sores all*
*over the body, mostly on the breasts. . . . Since the winters last a*
*long time there in the northern Urals, there were very few Sundays*
*off for us; we had to use these days to gather up in our bed covers*
*the snow we had shoveled around the barracks, and carry it down*
*to the riverbank; there we would get our water for washing and,*
*of course, due to the low temperatures, it would freeze in the tubs*
*after carrying it a few steps, so that we got back to the barracks*
*with ice shards.*

*Beginning in 1947 the food got a little better. We were paid*
*for our work, but not much was left from the cash payroll since*
*most of it was withheld as payment for "lodging," "heat," food,*
*etc. 500 grams of awful, doughy bread cost about 15 rubles.*
*Despite the relative improvement in the food, it was still bad*
*enough that most of us would supplement it by eating nettles,*
*potato peels and even grass. This led to bloating so that most of*
*us suffered from water on the knee, in the joints or in the face.*
*There was no medical facility available, and the excess body water*
*would cause the body sores to keep opening with torturous pain,*
*sticking to our clothes and thus getting even bigger. The body lice,*
*fleas and bedbugs we fought with all year long were yet another*
*torture. There was an almost continuous battle with skin ailments*
*like scabies, against which we could do nothing.*

*The majority of us women sustained bodily damage which*
*would last our whole lives. Since our bodies could not handle the*
*constant physical and emotional stress, even if we escaped work-*

*related accidents, many of us suffered from a lapse in the menstrual cycle for several years, not to mention worse things. The mental damage was even more lasting, the trauma has not left me since.*

*On December 22, 1949, we were once more loaded into trains at the freight station in Kungur. After 30 days of travel I was back in my hometown in Siebenbürgen. Even my emigration to West Germany a few years ago has not been able to wipe out the nightmare of those years in the Urals.*[24]

## The Testimony of Margarete Marquardt

It was not any better for the deportees from East Prussia and Pomerania. Frau Margarete Marquardt of Preussisch Holland, East Prussia, today residing in the Rhineland, gives her account.

*On February 9, 1945, we women with children age 14 and older were set on the march eastward. Then we were loaded into cattle cars. The cars remained closed for five days, nailed shut and totally black inside. During the whole trip, which lasted 29 days, we were let out at just one stop, where we were allowed to drink our fill of water at a lake. At that time 32 people out of 100 were already dead. When we arrived we were blinded by the sudden light from the opened door. It was difficult to walk because our legs were stiff and numb from squatting for so long.*[25]

## The Testimony of Hans Zeikau

Hans Zeikau of Elbing, East Prussia, tells of his imprisonment as a civilian technician in the armaments industry near Metgethen, East Prussia, and the ensuing deportation to the Urals.

*As soon as 1,000 people had been assembled, we were on-loaded. There were 700 women and 300 men ranging in age from 14 to 72 years, all East Prussian civilians. We were freighted off 40 to a car. After a 24-day trip we were off-loaded end of March 1945 in the Urals. We were put in a prison camp already holding German soldiers. They didn't believe their eyes when they saw old men and women coming into the camp. Only a short while ago a Russian training officer had told them: "Since the entry of the Red Army into East Prussia, the old*

*way of life there has continued as before!" Due to our lack of proper
clothing, much of it taken away from us previously, and because of the
poor provisions, the camp was hit hard by illness and disease. Eight to
15 people died each day. Our camp was Number 510 and lay about
20 km from Glasov. In winter we worked felling trees, in summer
cutting peat.*

*About mid-April I myself fell sick and had the fortune to be
sent to a hospital in Glasov on May 1. I had scarlet fever and
typhus. The medical treatment and general care were good. At the
beginning of August all the patients were returned to the main
camp because we were going to be released.*

*I saw here only a few healthy civilians from our transport out
of East Prussia. The strongest men and women were selected and
given forms to sign that said they pledged themselves to permanent
labor service in Russia. The people had no idea what they had
signed. They were lodged outside the camp and paid a few rubles
per day for their peat-cutting work.*

*On August 20, 1945, the rest of the survivors were shipped
out. Approximately 50 to 60% of all deportees were able to see
Frankfurt-on-the-Oder again.*[26]

## The Testimony of Paula D.

Frau Paula D. of Königsberg was also caught unaware by the Russians in
Metgethen and deported to the Urals.

*On February 28, 1945, we women of Bledau were separated from
our children and transported to the assembly camp at Carmitten.
I remained here for about three weeks. During this period we were
continually interrogated—they preferred taking us in the night—
and during the interrogations we were incessantly beaten and
subjected to bestial mistreatment. I'd rather not go into individual torture methods.*

*After three weeks we were brought to the penitentiary at
Tapiau. We sat here behind locked doors and barred windows,
shut from the outside world like criminals. At the beginning of
March we were loaded onto trains of cattle cars headed for Russia,
48 women in one cattle car. This terrible trip took about four
weeks. We ended up in the coal mines of Ruja in the Urals. Besides
many other jobs we had to do heavy men's work belowground.*

*Our guards were Poles who especially "distinguished" themselves in their mistreatment of our men. Getting punched, kicked and hit with a rifle butt was the order of the day.*

*We lay in underground barracks which were totally infested with bedbugs and lice. In order to get any peace at night we had to get out and sleep in the open air. Up to 40 people a day out of a starting contingent of 2,000 internees would die of starvation and typhoid fever. The dead were stripped naked and thrown into any open pit. For weeks on end I had to do the wash of the typhoid-infected inmates at the laundry without any disinfectant, almost the whole summer of 1945.*

*In October 1945, we were taken to a camp named Kistin in the Urals, which was occupied by German and other prisoners of war. All of the remaining women from the first camp were transferred here; there were about 200 of us. I estimate the losses in the first camp at more than 60%.*[27]

### The Testimony of Anna Reichrath

Survivors of these uprootings and abductions tried as best they could to rebuild their broken lives in the ruins of a broken Germany where they, too, were strangers. For them home was East Prussia, Silesia or the Banat—not Bavaria or Westfalia. Many simply did not adjust to the new environment and yearned for wider horizons: the United States, Canada or Australia. Among these is Anna Reichrath, born in the Romanian Banat, today an American citizen residing in Cincinnati, Ohio. On April 9, 1992 she told me:

*The Soviet Union took its reparations not only in money and goods, but also in human labour. That is how one morning in November 1944 my father and I were picked up and sent off to Russia. First they took us to a big hall and left us there for three days. Then we were forced into a cattle wagon with thrity other ethnic Germans, off to reconstruction work in Russia. After many days we were unloaded at a labor camp and quartered in barracks for 300 persons. The place was full of lice, the windows could not be opened. January 1945, and we had no light, no wood, no water!*

*The concentration camp was encompassed by a high barbed-wire fence and watched by guards from four towers. Three times a day we received a sauerkraut soup and a piece of bread made of ground chestnuts, which was so unbearably sour that we could hardly eat it.*

*I was assigned to a locomotive factory and had to work outside in the cold until my feet froze; then they put me to work in the kitchen. Because of the very bad food I became dystrophic, my body filled up with water, and I lost most of my teeth. We slept on wooden beds that were so hard that I would wake up numb. For heating we had to see how we could steal some wood from the factory. Almost every morning we found that one of us had died. We wondered who would be next.*

*After two years of tribulations, since so many of us were sick and could not work any longer, trains were organized to send us back—not to Romania, but to the German Democratic Republic. Still without any news of my husband or of my two children back home, I was released. I wrote to my mother-in-law and learned that my husband was in Austria. Miraculously, we were reunited. Then we had to get the children, but how? The children were still in Romania with their grandmother, and we had no papers or visa to return to the Banat. For my husband it would have surely meant arrest and imprisonment, maybe execution as a spy. But for a woman? I went and got through speaking Hungarian. Finally I was with my children—and in spite of the risks, we decided to escape, sleeping in the fields, crawling through the marshes, hiding in the forests. From Austria we then migrated to the United States.*

This chronicle of man's inhumanity to man could be continued. It was carried out systematically, as official Allied policy. Even if Americans and Britons did not directly perpetrate these abuses, we become responsible by virtue of joint decisions at Yalta and Potsdam. This "ethnic cleansing" of the *Volksdeutsche* constituted a crime against humanity, but the victims have remained unpitied and unknown. Seldom is there compassion for the vanquished. Seldom any justice in retribution.

# 6

# The Expellees in Germany —Yesterday and Today

Partake with others the living space on foreign soil,
Share graciously what you possess, that mercy you may also find.
. . . . . . . . . . . . . . . . . . . . . . . . . . . . . . . . .
Many deem it certain that in not too distant days
to cherished homelands they shall turn again
—thus do exiles oft caress their souls.
So lightly I shall not deceive myself in these sorrowful days that
presage continued sorrow.
Indeed, the bonds of the world have been unloosened; who shall
retie them?
Alone extreme Necessity, the direst Need before us.[1]

## REFUGEE MISERY AND ALLIED RELIEF MEASURES

The unimaginable misery suffered by the expellees in those years was barely known outside of Germany. Very few foreigners paid any attention or made any effort to establish privately funded assistance. Victor Gollancz was one of these few who attempted to publicize the catastrophe. He undertook several missions to the British Zone in Germany after which he followed up with reports to the British Parliament. His numerous books, in particular *Our Threatened Values* and *In Darkest Germany*, as well as many of his articles, contributed greatly to a degree of awareness of the expellee problem, to the launching of relief efforts and an increase in food rations.

Tons of American grain and potatoes were shipped to Germany. Then came the CARE packages. In a speech at Harvard University on June 7, 1947, American Secretary of State General George C. Marshall announced his plan for the reconstruction of post-war Europe. American aid was offered to all European states. Great Britain received the most, followed by France and Italy. But it had its greatest effect in Germany, for the assistance came at just the right time, when the need for physical and psychological reconstruction was at its highest point. The condition of the German economy was terrible, as could only be expected. Industrial production was but 27% of prewar volume. This alarming decline was due in part to the nearly total dismantling of German industry, a result of the politics at Potsdam. Its consequence was widespread unemployment.

What, then, of the expellees? Where were they supposed to work? Because of the lack of employment in postwar Germany, a number of American and French politicians affirmed that a liberal emigration policy to other countries, including the United States and Australia, offered a solution. As late as 1950 an American congressional committee recommended that 1 million German expellees should emigrate. Many did so, especially to the United States and Canada. However, most did not want to leave Germany forever.

The famous "economic miracle" made possible by the influx of Marshall Plan financing was equally grounded on the availability of skilled workers who had previously been without employment. Two important goals were attained in one stroke: rapid economic recovery and the integration of millions of expellees.

Even though most expellees came from predominantly agricultural regions, a considerable number of industries also were situated there, and many expellees brought their industrial expertise and technical skills with them.

Only by means of this economic miracle did the expellees have a chance to begin anew. They had many years of pain behind them. Now they could finally rebuild their lives and gaze hopefully into the future. Once they had obtained a job, their wish was to leave the barracks and emergency housing once and for all. Unfortunately, even in 1949 many expellees still had to live in group housing.

A Bavarian Red Cross report dated February 23, 1949, concerns the refugee camp community in the administrative district of Lower Bavaria/Oberpfalz.

## Report of the Bavarian Red Cross

*The privation and misery in refugee circles is sufficiently known to all offices. Prior to the currency reform [1948] it was a lack of commodities; after the reform it was for lack of money that these people, overwhelmed by chaos, were unable to find a way out or otherwise be in a position to start a new life. . . .*

*A number of men in the camps are unemployed; a number of women alone, their husbands either dead or still in foreign custody.*

*We want concise reports submitted by each camp citing those things it requires most urgently.*

> *The Refugee Camp Community in Dingolfing*
> *This camp consists of barracks where refugees are housed for lack of other arrangements. Oftentimes 2-3 families occupy a room 20 meters square.*
> *The lack of furnishings is especially noticeable here. One bed must hold two or three children or adults. Feather beds are scarce so that people living there must use the few blankets at their disposal to protect themselves from the cold. The wooden walls of the barracks are thin; storm windows unavailable.*
> *During the day beds are used as sitting places; there is not much else in the way of furniture. Because closets and wardrobes are unavailable, the few belongings are hung on walls. The majority of camp residents are welfare recipients. These support payments are by and large inadequate for family maintenance. Camp residents cannot acquire those things which would improve their lot because of the high costs involved. The camp is also home to persons with TB, invalids and elderly. In some families there is no breadwinner, making the wife bear the responsibility for her children alone. Each family in this camp suffers the same high level of want. There is no clothing, linen or shoes. All they could save of these and other possessions is in a rucksack, suitcase or bundle brought from their former homes. And after 4 years of camp life these few things are no longer fit for use. The greatest need, however, extends to feather beds and bedclothes.*
> *The sad pictures included with this report illustrate the misery barely imaginable even today:*

*In spite of the prevailing cold temperatures, laundry must be dried outdoors, since there is no room for it in the barracks.*

*Wooden outhouses and toilets are constructed with the most primitive methods. Several children in the refugee camp community in Dingolfing were without stockings even in winter, because their parents are unable to acquire them.*

*Two beds must serve five people. The walls, made of the usual plywood, are so damaged that the cold easily intrudes. The few items of clothing hanging on the walls are these people's entire wealth.*

*Refugee Camp Community in Sperlhammer*

*The barrack building is in very bad structural condition. This one building of ca. 100 square meters living space shelters five families, 32 persons total. The barrack exterior alone makes a desolate impression. The depth of privation was revealed after questioning the inhabitants and seeing the interior furnishing. In one room of 16 square meters, walls dripping wet, live two adults and seven children. The family's sleeping arrangements consist of three primitively assembled beds and one feather bed. The rest of the furnishings consists of a rotting wardrobe, a table, two benches, and one stool. The clothing of both adults and children is worse than inadequate. The father of the family receives 13 Marks per week invalid's pay, which must support a family of nine. Cardboard has been pasted on the walls as protection against the water leaking through them. A scantily clothed infant lay in a wash basket.*

*Conditions are similar for the other families in the camp at Sperlhammer. The inhabitants of this barrack will certainly begin to degenerate physically, mentally and morally if this want and privation continue, a situation which will affect the children far worse.*

## ECONOMIC AND SOCIAL INTEGRATION
## OF THE EXPELLEES

Former German Minister of Economics Dr. Erich Mende tells the story of the integration of expellees into the Federal Republic of Germany.

Dr. Erich Mende

*The adversities borne by the German populations of major cities, bombed to ruins and short on housing, had already taken the people to the edge of their tolerance; then came the influx of their countrymen from the East with their own set of demands. The country was burdened by more and more refugees, people bombed out of their homes and expellees. Friction between them and the native population was unavoidable, especially where cultural and religious differences would aggravate the contrasts.*

*The First German Bundestag in cooperation with the government of Chancellor Konrad Adenauer, based on a Christian Democrat, Free Democrat and German Party coalition, together viewed mastery of the expellee problem as one of their most important tasks. Additionally, they sought to guarantee the three fundamentals of life—food, shelter and work—for the 60 million West German citizens. Dr. Hans Lukaschek, a man familiar with the needs of those most affected, was named as minister of expellees. As an Upper Silesian who, at the beginning of the Weimar Republic, had played a major role in the election campaign of 1921, he had the confidence of wide circles in expellee matters. A first step was taken as early as November 29, 1949, with the enactment of a decree for resettlement of expellees, enabling the overburdened states of Bavaria, Lower Saxony and Schleswig-Holstein to direct several hundred thousand expellees to the states of Nordrhein-Westphalia, Baden-Wuerttemberg, Hessen and the Rheinland-Palatinate. Registration for resettlement was voluntary. The criteria for selection were: availability of jobs in targeted areas, family reunification, sharing a civil responsibility for those incapable of work, etc. This process continued in the years following, relieving the overburdened states while simultaneously directing valuable labor assets to the industrial regions of Nordrhein-Westphalia, Baden-Wuerttemberg and Hessen. The First New Housing Law enacted on April 24, 1950 encouraged construction of public housing with an immediate benefit, especially for the expellees. The law initiated an upsurge in new home construction. Homes and apartments by the million were built in the following years, a feat at which the whole world marveled.*

*On February 20, 1950, the Federal Maintenance Act for war victims went into effect. It restored the uniform maintenance of*

*war widows, orphans and disabled persons interrupted since
1945, contributing greatly to the relief of expellees in this cate-
gory. Then there were the laws of May 11, 1951, which redressed
National Socialist injustices for the benefit of members of the civil
service; furthermore, they regulated the legal recourse of persons
falling under Article 131 of the Constitution, providing a right
to social security for tens of thousands of expelled officials and
armed forces veterans as protection against circumstances of want
for which they were not responsible.*

*On September 5, 1951, the Federal Republic of Germany was
accepted into the advisory council of the United Nations High
Commissioner for Refugees, which gave a world forum to the
plight of German expellees.*

*The Equalization of Burdens Law of September 14, 1952 was
especially unique and effective. It spread the losses brought about
by the war, expulsion and currency reform among the entire
population. Compensation for the expellees, who were hardest hit,
ensued within the framework of the national economy. The total
benefits paid out was estimated at more than 114 billion Marks.
The equalization fund paid a total of 70.9 billion Marks from
the time the Immediate Relief Act of 1949 went into effect up to
December 31, 1968. Victims received 66.2 billion of this total.
In the years of economic growth which followed, a number of
amendments refined the equalization law to fit the changing
needs of fund recipients. The law is one of the greatest social
programs in German postwar democracy. Its fundamental, comprehensive structure is hitherto unique in the Western world.
Enactment of this law has made an essential contribution to the
social integration of the expellees, and to a political and human
reconciliation with a difficult past.*[2]

## THE CHARTER OF THE EXPELLEES

In the year 1949, which saw the birth of the Federal Republic of Germany, the
expellees began to organize politically. The two top expellee councils, namely
the United Eastern German Association and the Central Union of Expelled
Germans, adopted a "Magna Carta" of the Expellees at Göttingen in November
1949. This remarkable declaration undeniably assumes international signifi-

cance as a document very much in keeping with the goals of the United Nations. The time selected for its proclamation was the weekend of August 5-6, 1950, the weekend closest to the fifth anniversary of the end of the Potsdam Conference on August 2, 1945, when the protocol announcing the official Allied expulsion policy was issued.

Delegates from 30 leading groups assembled at the thermal center of Bad Cannstatt near Stuttgart. The charter was signed by their respective leaders. It was indeed symbolic that none of these public figures was chosen to proclaim the charter. This act would instead come from the mouth of an anonymous expellee, lending it greater significance, for he represented millions who had been affected by this fate.

On the following day, August 6, 1950, the charter's acceptance was recognized throughout the nation. On the Stuttgart Palace Square as well as in many other cities in Germany the charter was publicly proclaimed and universally accepted. It had thus received a kind of approval by plebiscite.

An American, Robert Hauser of Milwaukee, president of a coalition of German aid societies, was present at the mass proclamation in front of the palace ruins in Stuttgart, one among more than 100,000 people. He was so moved by this event that he distributed the text of the charter in the United States, thereby contributing to public awareness for the expellee problem.

What impressed him most of all was the fact that the charter was not a catalog of demands, a common trait among special interest groups: We demand, we claim, we expect. It spoke instead of the duties of the expellees and only thereafter of the rights they claimed.

The homeless expellees regarded the charter as their Constitution, an indispensable precondition for the creation of a free and united Europe.

A number of these duties and rights bear notice here. One of the central points in the charter was the first: The "expellees renounce revenge and retaliation . . ." Further, the expellees committed themselves to "support with all their strength any effort aimed at the creation of a unified Europe where its peoples can live without fear or coercion." This point was directed toward the future, and rightly so. Meanwhile Germany was reunified in 1989 and the European Community has become a reality. In 1993 a further big step toward political union is being taken.

Also, the expellees "shall by means of hard, tireless effort contribute to the reconstruction of Germany and Europe."

And this the expellees have done. They made a decisive contribution to the West German economic miracle. One cannot overlook financial preconditions created by the American Marshall Plan investments, some $1.4 billion worth; but the human preconditions, the capabilities of the people, and above all their will, these were eminently present.

Only after enumerating their obligations were certain demands made: "that the right to one's homeland as a God-given basic human right shall be both recognized and realized."

Moreover, even if this right could not be immediately realized, according to the expellees in 1950: "we do not then want to be condemned to the sidelines of inactivity, but rather work to create and effect in new, clarified form, an abiding, brotherly co-existence between all members of our society."[3]

The expellees further demanded: Equal rights as citizens, fair and just division of war debts, meaningful integration of all professions into the life of the German people and active participation in the process of the reconstruction of Europe.

As can be seen, the great significance of this charter lies in the fact that it is a program for action. And of still greater significance: The German expellees have lived by it.

To gauge its historical bearing, we should place ourselves in the time and situation in which this important commitment was made. Other nations feared, and with good reason, that a destroyed Germany in which millions of unemployed expellees were starving could turn into a time bomb. In fact it was Stalin's intention to bring about chaotic circumstances within Germany, where millions of uprooted, dispossessed and desperate people were crowded into a wrecked country. According to the Communist calculation, these millions would act as a social and political explosive. However, this reckoning did not come to pass.

Far from becoming terrorists in order to force the return of their homelands, the expellees preferred to take the path of peace and reconstruction. They successfully integrated themselves into the Federal Republic of Germany and contributed significantly to its economic revival.

> The old ways crumble, the times do change
> and new life springs out from the ruins.[4]

## The Testimony of Franz Hamm

One of the initiators and signatories to the Charter of the Expellees, Franz Hamm, born in 1900 in Neuwerbas in the Batschka, was secular president of the German Evangelical Church in southern Hungary. In an interview at his home in Bad Godesberg in 1981 he recalled:

> *You are certainly aware that after the total collapse of Germany it was especially difficult for the expellees, among others, to find a new beginning. Not only because they had lost their homelands*

*and practically all their material possessions, but also they had lost their identity. The great uncertainty in that time, when many counted on returning to their homelands, weighed heavily on the people. Added to this was the organizational ban imposed by the victorious powers. It prevented the formation of support groups which would at least look after the needs of the uprooted people. The coalitions of the major homeland churches played an important role in preventing chaos in Germany, for the native population did not have it much better than the millions who came from the East and Southeast. With the gradual relaxation and revocation of the organizational ban, a number of national groups were founded by the expellees: the Central Union of Expelled Germans; homeland associations; religious and charitable groups; scholarly and cultural societies; professional organizations; coalitions of refugees from the Soviet zone of occupation; political coalitions. Even among the youth there were signs of organization, such as German Youth from the East founded in 1951.*

*These various organizations were naturally unable to agree to a common set of by-laws, even though they had the experience of the expulsions and the obligations arising from them in common. In short order, practically every association, organization and committee came upon the idea of a unifying element, a declaration valid for all, concerning those problems which burdened them, and working out solutions to the questions which confronted the expellees in this society. The idea of a "Magna Carta" of the German expellees was born!*

*Each did his duty by it, which is apparent to anyone who carefully reads the charter.*

*I can tell you from my own experience that an overwhelming majority voted approval of the charter, indeed, it amounted to an approval by plebiscite. And what is especially important from my point of view; not only the expellees and refugees recognized its intent and demands! . . .*

*We should not forget that the expulsions, which sent millions packing, were obscured in the winds created by the great cataclysms at war's end and by anti-German propaganda. At the same time there were voices in the West drawing attention to the catastrophe raging in Germany, made only worse by the expellee problem. A sociologist in Chicago, an official in a displaced persons organization, pointed out that the world shared a responsibility for the plight of German expellees, and demanded help in finding a solution. It was a problem, he said, which could not be left to the Germans alone. Later, in the fall of 1950, at an assembly he had called and in the presence of an expellee delegation, he declared that a ruined, starved, economically depressed and divided Germany had nevertheless within three years overcome the problems posed by millions of people streaming into the country. It was the miracle of the century!*

*The Charter is the promise of the expellees to all the world. We spoke this promise at a time when new pathways were being sought. For example, an echo came unexpectedly from India, which recognized in that promise its own policy of nonviolence, the same nonviolence with which the expellees sought to reach their goals!*

It is valid to note that the public expression of renunciation against revenge did not merely stem from a condition of weakness. It has been maintained ever since, and prevails as Germany emerged to a respected position of economic and political power. The 1991 German-Polish and 1992 German-Czechoslovak Treaties of Friendship and Good Neighborliness are an example of this willingness to cooperate and build a peaceful future together. The vicious circle has thus been broken.

## THE HOMELAND IN THE HEARTS OF THE EXPELLEES
### (*HEIMATBEWUSSTSEIN*)

The following two poems show that renunciation of revenge and retribution does not mean that the expellees have forgotten their homelands or given up the hope they or their children or grandchildren might one day return. A Sudeten German writer from the Egerland, Dr. Wilhelm Pleyer, gives an example in this profession of faith:

### Prayer
We came as sowers
To a barren wilderness:
The soil furrowed
Deeply by our plows.
We cut down trees,
The land was cleared,

From out of wilderness
Our homeland grew.
We mined the mountains
Deep for ore.
We toiled to make
Their wealth to pour
Into the forges glowing,
The chimneys rising, growing;
As did your cathedral, Lord,
High above us all.
Now driven out are we,
The sowers and craftsmen;
Our homeland a prison—
Such is our fate.
Hear us, Lord,
Our faith calls to Thee:
Redeem the despoiled lands
And lead us back home![5]

Many expellees have expressed their faith in the homeland through poetry, short stories and novels.[6] The next poem was written by Walter Vorbach, a successful lawyer, an expellee from Gablonz, Sudetenland, long since integrated into his West German community, Heidelberg. He received his doctorate at the German University in Prague in 1934.

### Bohemia
The others came and said
We had no part in you,
Produced their letters, figures, stamps,
To prove they called us to their land.
Yes, they had their tents here first
And thus they called you Their
Bohemia.
We quibbled not over the figures,
Did not inquire since when
Bohemia knew her Germans:
We stood here—
No need for words.
And were we slaughtered all,
The stone prayers of your Cathedrals

Would have sung our love for you:
Bohemia.
Now they have you for themselves,
Alone.
And yet, do they enjoy their role?
With Charles, Wenceslas and Witiko,
You had been Europe's heart.
And will you be this heart once more?
Knows God alone.[7]

Who can deny these feelings when an expellee, in tranquil moments, recalls the words of Rainer Maria Rilke:

How deeply move me
these Bohemian folkways
that steal into the heart,
And make it heavy!
When a child softly sings
While weeding potato beds—
His song haunts your dreams
So late into the night.
Even if you travel far
to foreign lands, still
that melody resounds in
yonder years in your very soul.[8]

Among the German expellees we also recognize major names of German postwar literature. Günter Grass, for instance, was born in 1927 in Danzig, where the plot of his most famous novel *The Tin Drum* (1959) unwinds. From the perspective of a young boy, distrustful of the adult world around him, Grass masterfully paints a bizarre canvas of the petit-bourgeois society drawn into the maelstrom of Nazism, war and destruction. This novel, the first of what is frequently called his "Danzig trilogy," was followed by *Cat and Mouse* (1963) and *Dog Years* (1965).

Another major author is Siegfried Lenz, born in the town of Lyck in East Prussia in 1926. In his book *The Heritage* (1978), Lenz weaves a nostalgic sixty-year tale about a museum of local history in the Masurian Lake district of East Prussia. In the end, the museum burns to ashes, and with it the material souvenirs of the life and tribulations of a small town. It remains for human recollection, for the written and spoken word, to preserve the past for future generations.

Yet another East Prussian author is Arno Surminski, born in Jäglack in 1934, whose novels *Jokehnen* (1974), a family saga, and *Kudenow* (1978), a story of the integration of expellees in Holstein, West Germany, radiate a positive and forward-looking attitude while still recalling with fondness the East Prussian countryside and traditions.

Belonging to the same generation, we recall the prominent political analyst and historian, Christian Graf von Krockow, born in Pomerania in 1927, whose books *Pommern—Bericht aus einem verschwiegenen Land* and *Heimat— Erfahrungen mit einem deutschen Thema* have made a significant contribution to a liberal understanding of the Nazi catastrophe and postwar reconstruction and reconciliation with Germany's eastern neighbors.

The Cultural Foundation of the German Expellees, an organization in Bonn, has collected the literary works of many expellees in a colorful anthology published in 1985 under the title *Vertriebene...Literarische Zeugnisse von Flucht und Vertreibung*, which contains excerpts from novels as well as touching poems and essays by Hans Bergel, Horst Bienek, Nelly Däs, Marion Gräfin Dönhoff, Peter Huchel, Heribert Losert, Heinz Piontek, Gerhart Pohl, Ruth Storm, Monika Taubitz, Ilse Tielsch and Ernst Wiechert, among others.

Let us now hear a younger voice, an Upper Silesian named Josef Resner who resettled in the former West Germany in 1979 and today resides in Freiburg im Breisgau, where he also completed his university studies.

## The Testimony of Josef Resner

*I was born in March 1955, the tenth year of Polish administration in my homeland. The village in which I was born is called Rodenau, though today it can only be called by its Polish name. It lies in Upper Silesia, in the county of Tost-Gleiwitz.*

*I am German and have always felt as such, same as my family. Our ancestors have lived for generations in this region of eastern Germany.*

*We moved to Preiskretscham two years after my birth, a city on the so-called High Road (from the west via Breslau-Cracow to the east) in the vicinity of Gleiwitz. Preiskretscham was incorporated under German law as early as 1260. I began my schooling there, eventually graduating from two more schools in Gleiwitz.*

*In early childhood German was spoken quite frequently at home. But my parents had been warned by a friendly Polish teacher that they should speak more Polish with me, so as not to hurt my chances for a future, and because of anti-German sentiment among some other teachers. Additionally, there was fear of possible reprisals. (At that time the use of the German mother tongue was officially prosecuted.) Consequently, I heard less and less German at home, and I forgot much of it. In Upper Silesia, where several hundred thousand Germans still live, there were no opportunities to study German in schools, not even as a foreign language elective. Yet everywhere else in Poland one could elect and study it as a foreign language. It was primarily Polish children who had the option. Not until I was in Cracow, during my undergraduate years, did I first become aware of the unequal treatment afforded German youth. Back home I thought the situation there was the same for the whole country.*

*The attitude of our Polish neighbors regarding the occasional use of the German language varied. There were cases marked by tolerance, or indifference, or outright hateful reaction. For example, when German folk songs were sung at birthdays or other family get-togethers; besides, the Poles generally celebrate name days contrary to the Germans, who celebrate birthdays.*

*In order to understand the language situation of the German generation born under Polish administration, and the attendant identity crisis occasionally faced by this generation, it is important to understand that everything German is continuously portrayed as evil, based on actual or imaginary misdeeds committed by Germans throughout history, especially during World War II, but also as far back as the time of the Teutonic Order of Knights. The Polish media miss no opportunity to depict the Germans as "eternal" criminals. Television will often have films showing Germans in a negative light, the subject matter based on the mentioned historical periods. In class, primarily Polish and History, the Germans are represented as a nation of conquerors and aggressors, notions which are popularized in the press. The basic tenor is characterized by the following slogans: "Here we were, here we are, here we stay"—meaning the eastern German regions. Or: "These regions are reclaimed property." The brutal expulsion of the Germans from their ancestral homelands is denied as an historical fact in schools and in public opinion. The explanation for the removal of the German population from the eastern provinces is glib and simple: A criminal people, they fled when faced with the just conquerors of these regions. The motive for the flight is supposedly obvious, namely, fear of a deserved punishment.*

*Based on this evidence, the question can justifiably be asked, who wants to be put on display as a member of a criminal nation? I believe*

*it is for this reason, and not at all surprising, that many of our young
resettlers in Germany have problems at first with language, and even
with identity. The German heritage in their homelands was and is still
given no opportunity for development.*

*Back in the 1950s my father had already wrestled with the
idea of emigration. At that time the chances for such were slim.
The matter was put aside. Besides, he and many other Germans
in Upper Silesia had hoped that the circumstances which arose
after the war might one day change. A turning point came with
the so-called Eastern Treaties of 1970-72, though they dealt in
no way with the minority rights issues of Germans in the eastern
territories. But they did offer thousands a new chance to emigrate.
To put it bluntly, what helped were the billions in credit given
Poland by West Germany.*

*The motive for our departure was determined by the loss of hope in
any guarantee of minority rights, and to withdraw ourselves and the
children from forced "polonization," to live a normal life as Germans.
Anyway, for many years I had been planning to leave for West
Germany, even if alone, by emigration or flight. We have many
relatives in Germany who had been here for some time, a number of
them since 1945. Except for me, my whole family left for the transfer
camp in Friedland in December 1977. I had decided to come later.
My reasons were the following: First, I wanted to make a personal,
lifetime decision for myself while "over there"; and second, I had but
four semesters to go at Cracow to complete my studies, which I could
then continue in West Germany.*

*I was able to visit my family and relatives in West Germany in late
summer, 1978. On July 5, 1979, I arrived in the Federal Republic of
Germany for good. An important date in my life. Unlike the rest of my
family, I did not have to live in the transfer camp; my parents already
had an apartment where I now had a new home. After a ten-month
language course I was able to begin studies in the following semester.
My father was also very lucky. After not quite two months he found a
good job.*

*Being recognized as Germans by the resident population has not
been a problem for us. My fellow students regard me as German.
Freiburg, the Federal Republic, became my second homeland.*

This late resettler, (*Spätaussiedler,* a hint of forced departure, of little choice
is implied by the term) is still a member of the expellee generation. He was

personally, directly affected by the polonization of Upper Silesia, an experience that has left its mark on him.

How do the children of expellees see themselves even though they were born in West Germany? Do they regard themselves as eastern Germans? A young Danube Swabian interviewed in 1985 introduces himself in the following account.

## The Testimony of Mathias Weifert

*I was born on May 18, 1960 in Schweinfurt, Lower Saxony. I am a Danube Swabian. My father's side of the family comes from Pantschowa in the Banat (until 1920 Hungary, today Yugoslavia). The last place in which my father resided there was Temeschburg (also Hungary until 1920, today called Timisoara in Romania). My mother's family originates in Miltenberg (my home town) in Lower Saxony.*

*I learned about the Banat homeland through the many stories told by my father since I was a small child. As I grew older I became more involved with research into my family history, its origins and accomplishments in the Banat. Because of this I was able to discover living relatives in Landshut, Munich and Vienna, relations we had known nothing about.*

*It was primarily my mother who taught me to appreciate and practice traditions and customs. During the time of my civilian service in Wuerzburg I came upon a Banat youth group made up entirely of young resettlers from the present-day Romanian part of the Banat. I was accepted as the only non-resettled member.*

*Based on my experience in cultural and youth group activity, I was able to eventually establish the Danube Swabian Youth group in 1982. This organization, of which I have since become chairman, embraces the new generations whose roots lie in all the major Danube Swabian territories (southwest Hungarian Central Mountains, Swabian Turkey in Hungary, Batschka, Slavonia-Syrmia, Banat and Sathmar), and consists of approximately 1,000 members, both emigrants and those born later in West Germany. Ages range from 6 to 29 years.*

*Besides my hobby, the cultivation of Danube Swabian folkways. . . . I am also deeply involved with the fate of my ethnic group still living in the old homelands as well as here in Germany.*

*I try to combine my hobby with my education. For example, my dissertation for the state exam in geography concerned "The Evolution of Temeschburg, Capital of the Banat." I am studying at the University of Erlangen-Nuremberg to be a high school teacher in geography, economics and sociology. By my efforts I hope that I can at least make a small contribution to the preservation of Danube Swabian culture.*

In conclusion, let us listen to one more young voice. Ansgar Graw, born on June 20, 1961, in Essen, is a member of the Young East Prussian Association. What do these young people desire? Here is his position.

## The Testimony of Ansgar Graw

*I was born in a divided country 16 years after the war. The older I became, the more conscious I was of the anomaly this situation in Germany represented.*

*My father is an expellee from the East Prussian Ermland; my mother comes from Westphalia. I myself was born in the German "coal bin," grew up in the Rhineland and later went to northern Germany for job reasons. I could not therefore develop a true East Prussian identity. But I do identify myself as a German, in this, the Germany I know as my fatherland; and to me it is self-evident that the homeland of my father, as well as all of historic eastern and middle Germany, belong to this identity.*

*For this reason I am active in the Young East Prussian Association. I thereby recognize the culture and history of this German province which, since 1945 has been under Polish, i.e., Russian administration.*

*In 1990 we Germans finally got the right to self- determination, to reestablish national unity in peace and freedom. For me this was never merely a precept found in the preamble of our Constitution, it was also a deep and profound desire; and so I felt very happy when, in November 1989, the Wall came crashing down. At the same time it was obvious to me that the enactment of these rights for Germans need not lead to new injustice, to new expulsions, this time for Poles and Russians. The expellees have already sworn themselves against revenge and retribution in 1950. This applies in equal terms to the younger generations.*

*Because of this we must find different solutions to the question of former German territories, the provinces of East and West Prussia, Pomerania and Silesia. Questions relative to the future of these regions are not primarily concerned with changes, yet again, in state frontiers.*

*Among our immediate political goals must be increased media, and above all, educational attention given to the flight and expulsion in the East, the cultural legacies of East Prussia and Pomerania, and last but not least, to the plight of those Germans still living in the eastern German territories. A demand for such truthful and comprehensive information on subjects so far ignored cannot be branded as an act of revenge.*

*I have visited the former eastern German provinces many times, most often East Prussia. Contacts with Germans living there, and more often the discussions with Poles in the south and Russians in the north, were very informative. I am convinced it will be possible to one day reach a true, lasting and comprehensive reconciliation with them, preceded by a just solution to contested interests. That solution should embrace the right of return for refugees, the right for German expellees to resettle there, in a broad, European context; and the right to compensation for lost property. The regions of expulsion could thus develop into a bridge between Germans and Poles, Russians and the Baltic peoples. Any other position would give the final word to the injustice of the expulsions, annexation and division. And that would once again raise a worldwide danger of new expulsions and annexations. For then any state would reckon with the fact that it need only hold on for a few years, at most a few decades, after annexation of a neighboring state and expulsion of its population. After such time has passed public opinion will "accept the reality" of the situation, and thereby contribute to the injustice.*

One might properly ask just how long someone remains an expellee. One generation? Two? Ansgar Graw has shown us what it is all about: a feeling of identity, of commitment to one's roots. As long as these young Germans profess to be from East Prussia, Pomerania or Silesia, as long as they cultivate their traditions, they belong to the community of expellees.

Many of these young people travel to Silesia and Pomerania these days, to the Sudetenland, all over East and Southeast Europe, in order that they might get to know the land of their parents and grandparents. Then there are the homesick tourists who want to see the old homelands again, there, where once the wheat in the field grew higher, where the smell of the land was once stronger, familiar.

> The wind traversed the fields,
> through softly waving grain,
> And forests mildly rustling.
> How starry was that night!
> My soul outspread
> Its all-embracing wings,
> Flew o'er the tranquil land
> And wafted to its home.[9]

Yes, once again there are Germans "on loan" in the East. The tourists who, since the Treaties of Warsaw (1970) and Prague (1972), and more so since the Friendship and Good Neighborliness Treaties of 1991 experience the profound joy of return to their beloved soil. The rivers and mountains are still there—but seldom are the cemeteries, where generations of eastern Germans lay buried. Following German reunification, the Oder-Neisse frontier was formally recognized in the German-Polish Treaty of November 18, 1990. The Germans press no further claims over Silesia or East Prussia. But the process of European integration will no doubt lead to greater economic and cultural exchange. Perhaps a European region of Silesia will gradually emerge. Indeed, the stones there speak both Polish and German.

## RECENT ARRIVALS: DELAYED EXPELLEES

German visitors in Pomerania and Silesia, in the Sudetenland, Hungary and Romania, do not encounter just native Poles, Czechs, Hungarians and Romanians. They also find many Germans and their descendants living there. Many Germans with vocational skills were not expelled from 1945 to 1949, but were allowed to remain in their homelands. It is estimated that, at present, 800,000 Germans live in the former eastern provinces of Germany and in Old Poland; approximately 100,000 in Czechoslovakia; 200,000 in Hungary; 100,000 in Romania; not to mention the 2 million still living throughout Russia, Belarus and the Ukraine.

This fact represents an enduring human problem, for the Germans living in eastern European countries do not want to surrender their cultural legacy. They wish to cultivate the German language, educate their children in German schools. Their existence as an ethnic minority in their ancestral homelands has not been easy. Added to this is the desire for family reunification. Many of them have close relatives in Germany.

For this reason many Germans leave the countries of Eastern Europe. Granted, they are not "expellees" in the literal sense. But their fate is inseparable from that of the expellees. In one sense they can be described as "delayed expellees," because following the expulsion of 90% of the German majority population, they remained as unwanted minorities, whose human rights were not respected by the new majorities. They were second class citizens under great pressures to abandon their identity and assimilate. The continued existence of German communities, the exercise of their own culture was made almost impossible; for decades they were discriminated against and intimidated, and in some countries they were fined or criminally prosecuted for speaking German or trying to teach it to their children. Burdened by the prevailing consequences of the massive upheaval, many would try again and again to emigrate to West Germany. In fact, after the actual expulsions were concluded in 1949, more than 2 million eastern Germans managed to go to the West.

After the collapse of the Soviet bloc and the reunification of Germany, new hope has arisen for the German minorities in Eastern Europe. On the basis of the Conference on Security and Cooperation in Europe and the continued "Helsinki Process," the rights of minorities have been internationally recognized. They are now guaranteed through bilateral German-Polish and German-Czechoslovak agreements.

# Epilogue

The most grievous violation of the right based on historical evolution and of any human right in general is to deprive populations of their right to occupy the country where they live by compelling them to settle elsewhere. The fact that the victorious powers decided at the end of World War II to impose this fate on hundreds of thousands of human beings and, what is more, in a most cruel manner, shows how little they were aware of the challenge facing them, namely, to reestablish prosperity and, as far as possible, the rule of law.

-Albert Schweitzer upon accepting the
Nobel Price for Peace in Oslo on November 4, 1954)[1]

The flight and expulsion of so many millions of Germans from the territories East of the Oder and Neisse rivers, and from the Sudetenland and Southeast Europe, cannot be appreciated as a historical event by means of cold statistics. The fate of each individual person must be kept in mind. The victims of the expulsion were people no different from us. They suffered and starved as individual human beings, not nameless subtotals in some statistical column. They were victims just like the Polish officers in the Katyn Forest, or the gypsies liquidated by Nazi hit squads, or the Jews murdered at Auschwitz. For those affected—no matter whether Pole, gypsy, Jew or German—being a victim meant that their personal existence was extinguished, often under circumstances of unbearable torment. All fell victim to injustices that can never be redressed.

It is not inappropriate here to recall a contemporary voice, that of Robert Murphy, the political adviser of the American Military Government in Berlin, who against the background of chaos and profound human misery wrote an urgent memorandum to the State Department on October 12, 1945:

> In the Lehrter Railroad station in Berlin alone our medical author-ities state an average of ten have been dying daily from exhaustion, malnutrition and illness. In viewing the distress and despair of these wretches, in smelling the odor of their filthy condition, the mind reverts instantly to Dachau and Buchenwald. Here is retribution on a large scale, but practiced not on the *Parteibonzen,* but on women and children, the poor, the infirm. . . .
>
> Knowledge that they are victims of a harsh political decision carried out with the utmost ruthlessness and disregard for the humanities does not cushion the effect. The mind reverts to other mass deportations which horrified the world and brought upon the Nazis the odium which they so deserved. Those mass deportations engineered by the Nazis provided part of the moral basis on which we waged war and which gave strength to our cause. Now the situation is reversed. We find ourselves in the invidious position of being partners in this German enterprise and as partners inevitably sharing the responsibility. . . . It would be most unfortunate were the record to indicate that we are *particeps* to methods we have often condemned in other instances.[2]

The survivors of this tragedy cannot just blot out their memories. Thou-sands of women who had been repeatedly raped had to bear the physical and psychological scars for their entire lives. Surely this is one of history's terrible chapters, one that has not yet been sufficiently studied in its psychological and sociological aspects. If one could take the place of a survivor, truly feel his or her pain, know what it means to endure physical violence and the sight of one's entire family utterly humiliated and then murdered, as did Frau Marie Neumann, the thought of going on to lead a "normal" life would not come easy.

The integration of expelled Germans has been accomplished. The unimagin-able sufferings of the war generation have in the meantime been pushed aside, if not substantially forgotten. When we consciously look back into the recent past, however, we must not trivialize the losses. They were colossal. Future generations shall recognize and value the achievements of the Eastern Germans, of the expellees and their descendants, of so many men and women who accepted great suffering and sacrifice for the sake of peace, who renounced vengeance and retaliation.

It would have been good if the fate of the German expellees had pressed upon the conscience of all politicians in Europe and thus served as a warning, in the hope that other nations would be spared the tragedy of ethnic annihilation. But we still live in a world in which man's inhumanity to man knows no end. The optimism we all felt when Gorbachev's policies of *glasnost* and *perestroika* took hold has been followed by the sobering knowledge that considerable tensions persist in Europe that have led to armed conflict and bloodshed in many former republics of the once-mighty Soviet Union, and in states once associated with it, notably the former Yugoslavia.

With the dismantlement of Marxism-Leninism, we are witnessing a resurgence of old nationalisms, as reflected in ethnic and religious rivalries. Once again men, women and children are leaving their homes in panic, while others fear persecution and eventual expulsion. We see that even the gruesome example of World War II and its aftermath has not deterred politicians from pursuing intolerant and xenophobic policies that have already led to the displacement of hundreds of thousands of persons and may result in further refugee movements. What we would have considered an anachronism, the repugnant policy of "ethnic cleansing," is being implemented today in the former Yugoslavia, particularly in Bosnia-Herzegovina. Why such aberrations are taking place cannot be answered here. But it seems to this writer that if the German experience had been studied more closely instead of being ignored, or deemed a taboo subject, today's politicians would have had useful parameters to judge the current situation.

The United Nations and the Conference for Security and Cooperation in Europe have devoted much effort to solving the tragedy in the former Yugoslavia, a country born as a result of the Paris Peace Conference that ended World War I. Czechoslovakia, another country that was established in the wake of the dismemberment of the Austro-Hungarian monarchy, separated into two sovereign states on January 1, 1993—fortunately without violence. The observer cannot but wonder whether Europe is returning to the power constellation that existed prior to World War I. If so, what other developments can be expected, and will those developments respect the human rights of the peoples concerned?

The present generation of Germans is fully occupied with the challenge of reunification. German politicians do not indicate any desire to see the old provinces of East Prussia, Pomerania or Silesia returned. Indeed, since the years of Chancellor Willy Brandt and the policy of reconciliation with Germany's eastern neighbors, exemplified not just by Brandt's genuflection in Warsaw in 1970 but by the *de jure* recognition of the Oder Neisse frontier, there is no question of German ambitions in the East. Still, it is not easy to predict history, and we have witnessed how the aspirations of peoples do evolve. Thus, it is not altogether unthinkable that in 10 or 20 years time a German government may wish to negotiate with Poland for a partial revision of the Oder-Neisse frontier. Indeed, if Stalin's works have collapsed and his statues have tumbled, is it not an anomaly that such an important legacy still prevails, the German-Polish frontier Stalin personally invented and imposed on the Western Allies in 1945? Thus it should surprise no one if one day the ancient Pomeranian town of Stettin, on the west bank of the Oder River, returns to Germany. Indeed, the Helsinki Final Act envisages the possibility of peaceful change of frontiers through mutual agreement.[3] Accordingly, Germany could conceivably negotiate for the return of some of its pre–World War II provinces, possibly against further economic and technical aid to Poland.

Similarly, Germany could negotiate with the Russian Federation for the return of the northern half of East Prussia, which Stalin annexed to the Soviet Union at the end of World War II, ostensibly pursuant to Article 6 of the Potsdam Protocol. Following the demise of the Warsaw Pact, the reestablishment of full sovereignty in Poland and the independence of Lithuania, the Russian Federation has been territorially separated from East Prussia; moreover, Russia does not have any significant historical, economic or strategic interests there. Thus it would not be inconceivable for Germany, at some future date, to engage in peaceful negotiations with an aim to regain its sovereignty over a territory whose German history goes back to the year 1226, and whose culture is forever associated with the names of Immanuel Kant, Johann Gottfried Herder and E. T. A. Hoffmann.

European developments in the post-Soviet era will be increasingly determined by the Council of Europe, which is guided not only by economic considerations but just as much by a genuine commitment to human rights as laid down in the 1950 European Convention on Human Rights and Fundamental Freedoms. No major decisions are taken today in Europe without reference to this convention, and political and social developments in the area, including the abuses and atrocities committed against civilians during the armed conflict in the former Yugoslavia, are judged in its light.

Among those human rights that Europeans hold dear is the right to one's homeland. This very right, which the German expellees invoke for themselves and which is a central demand of their 1950 charter, also applies to the two generations of Poles and Czechs who have been born in and have cultivated the lands that were formerly the homeland of East Prussians and Sudetenlanders. The right to the homeland of these Poles and Czechs must be respected, and any scheme that would return Germans to these territories must take the rights of the native Polish and Czech populations into account. Bearing in mind the history of twentieth century German-Polish and German-Czech tensions, it is important to stress that no leader of the German expellees has ever proposed an expulsion of Poles or Czechs from the territories in question. Such an expulsion would, of course, violate Protocol 4 to the European Convention on Human Rights, which prohibits collective expulsions, and to which Germany is a party. But more fundamentally, a European consensus has been reached that increased integration and interdependence must be the rule in the twenty-first century. Thus, even if there is a gradual return to pre–World War I demographic conditions, this must not be achieved under the banner of nineteenth-century nationalism, but rather under the banner of human rights, cultural pluralism and respect for minority rights.

The new order emerging in Europe as a result of the gradual democratization of Eastern Europe will not be a German new order but rather a European order based on the principles of equality and human rights. This new order has been placed under the supervision of the Council of Europe and of the Conference on Security and Cooperation in Europe, in which the United States also plays a leading role. Thus there is every reason to expect that all major decisions in Europe will henceforth be taken by consensus and upon general deliberation by all parties concerned.

I hope to have shown that population transfers, past, present and (not, it is hoped) future, must be seen from the perspective of human rights. Indeed, the phenomenon of forced resettlement is not limited to the German experience but continues to threaten and affect other peoples throughout the world. Expulsion, however, has not proven itself to be a viable solution of tensions associated with national or ethnic minorities. The recognition and respect of minority rights is. In this connection I welcome the adoption, on December 18, 1992, by the United Nations General Assembly of a Declaration on the Rights of Persons Belonging to National or Ethnic, Religious and Linguistic Minorities.[4] Much progress is being achieved by the United Nations and the Conference on Security and Cooperation in Europe in the field of the effective protection of minority rights. Ultimately, the key to the solution of the problems discussed in this book lies in the acceptance of the simple fact that we all possess the same *dignitas humana* and in the recognition that the best policy to avoid conflict with neighbors is to get to know them, to intensify cultural and other exchanges so as to discard once and for all the prejudices and stereotypes that have caused and continue to cause so much needless suffering in Europe and the world.

# APPENDIX

## Populations Census Before Flight and Expulsion
## German Population, 1939

| | | |
|---|---|---|
| Eastern Territories of the German Reich | | 9,575,000 |
| East Prussia | 2,473,000 | |
| eastern Pomerania | 1,883,000 | |
| eastern Brandenburg | 642,000 | |
| Silesia | 4,577,000 | |
| Czechoslovakia | | 3,477,000 |
| Baltic States and Memeland | | 250,000 |
| Danzig | | 380,000 |
| Poland | | 1,371,000 |
| Hungary | | 623,000 |
| Yugoslavia | | 537,000 |
| Romania | | 786,000 |
| **SUBTOTAL*** | | **16,999,000** |
| Gains (births minus deaths), 1939-45 | | 659,000 |
| **TOTAL** | | **17,658,000** |
| War Losses, 1939-45 | | 1,100,000 |
| Losses through flight and expulsion | | 2,111,000 |
| **TOTAL LOSSES** | | **3,211,000** |

*2 million in the Soviet Union not included.

Thus, in the territories subjected to expulsion, one of every five Germans in the 1939 census died in battle or perished in the aftermath.

## Flight and Expulsion (1945-1950)

### Refugees and Expellees

| | | |
|---|---|---|
| From the eastern territories | | |
| of the German Reich | 6,944,000 | |
| From Czechoslovakia | 2,921,000 | |
| From other countries | 1,865,000 | |
| SUBTOTAL | | 11,730,000 |
| | | |
| Remainder Populations | | |
| In the eastern territories | | |
| of the German Reich | 1,101,000 | |
| In Czechoslovakia | 250,000 | |
| In other countries | 1,294,000 | |
| SUBTOTAL | | 2,645,000 |
| | | |
| Civilians deported to Soviet Union | 72,000 | |
| as prisoners of war in 1950 | | |
| (presumed to be alive) | | |
| | | |
| TOTAL | | 14,447,000 |

### Dead or Missing in Flight and Expulsion

| | | |
|---|---|---|
| In the eastern territories | | |
| of the German Reich | 1,225,000 | |
| In Czechoslovakia | 267,000 | |
| In other countries | 619,000 | |
| | | |
| SUBTOTAL | | 2,111,000 |

### Sum Total of German Expellees and Their Offspring, 1966 (est.)

| | |
|---|---|
| In West Germany (FRG) | 10,600,000 |
| In East Germany (GDR) | 3,500,000 |
| In Austria and other Western countries | 500,000 |

Source: German Federal Ministry for Expellees, 1967. Between 1950 and 1992 more than 2.8 million ethnic Germans migrated to Germany from the East European states. Some 68% of the expellees settled in the former Federal Republic of Germany; 25% in the former German Democratic Republic; 3% in Austria and 4.6% (some 750,000) in the United States, Canada and Australia.
It is estimated that in 1992 more than 3.2 million ethnic Germans still live in Eastern Europe:
In Poland approximately 800,000
In the Czech and Slovak Republics 100,000
In Hungary 200,000
In Romania 100,000
In the Russian Federation 1,000,000
In the Former Soviet Republics 1,000,000

# NOTES

## Note to Introduction

1. Eva Krutein, *Eva's War, A True Story of Survival* (Albuquerque, N.M., 1990); Regina Shelton, *To Lose a War* (Carbondale, Ill., 1980).

## Notes to Chapter 1

1. Henry Wadsworth Longfellow, *Evangeline,* contained in Charles Eliot (ed.), *The Harvard Classics,* Vol. 42 (New York, 1938), p. 1300.
2. Translation by John Koehler.
3. *Es war ein Land,* Translation by John Koehler and Alfred de Zayas.
4. Wir sind durch Not und Freude
   gegangen Hand in Hand,
   vom Wandern ruhen wir
   nun überm stillen Land.

   Rings sich die Täler neigen,
   es dunkelt schon die Luft,
   zwei Lerchen nur noch steigen
   nachträumend in den Duft.

   Tritt her und lass sie schwirren,
   bald ist es Schlafenszeit,
   dass wir uns nicht verirren
   in dieser Einsamkeit.

   O weiter, stiller Friede!
   So tief im Abendrot.
   Wie sind wir wandermüde—
   ist dies etwa der Tod?

   (Translation by Alfred de Zayas.)

5. Gerhart Pohl, *Gerhart Hauptmann and Silesia* (Grand Forks, N.D., 1962,) pp. 65 et seq.
6. Ibid., p. 67.
7. Goethe, *Faust* II, Act III, V. 9931-38.

## Notes to Chapter 2

1. Congressional Record, Senate, January 8, 1918, pp. 680-681; *Foreign Relations of the United States*, 1918, vol. I, Supp. I, p.112.
2. United States Department of State, *Papers Relating to the Foreign Relations of the United States, The Paris Peace Conference, 1919*, vol. 12, p. 273.
3. Ibid., p. 274.
4. Permanent Court of International Justice, Series B. No. 6, pp. 6 et seq.. In fact, over 1 million Germans left the provinces of Posen and West Prussia (the Corridor) as a result of various coercions. I studied many of the German petitions and protests filed with the League of Nations, at the League of Nations Archives in Geneva. See also E. Kulischer, *Europe on the Move* (New York, 1948), pp. 134-5; H. Rauschning, *Die Entddeutschung Posens und Westpreussens* (Berlin, 1930). Also Herbert von Truhardt, *Völkerbund und Minderheiten-petitionen* (Leipzig, 1931); H. Pieper, *Die Minderheitenfrage und das Deutsche Reich 1919-1934* (Hamburg, 1974).
5. Arnold Toynbee, "Czechoslovakia's German Problem," *The Economist*, 10 July 1937, p. 72.
6. *Documents on British Foreign Policy*, 1919-1939, 3rd series, vol. 2, pp. 675-7.
7. Upon returning from Munich, Chamberlain addressed a cheering crowd outside 10 Downing Street. He spoke of "peace with honour," and the crowd wanted to believe it. John Wheeler-Bennett, *Munich: Prologue to Tragedy* (New York, 1948), p. 181.
8. A. Toynbee, "A Turning Point in History," *Foreign Affairs* (January 1939), p. 316. See also *The Times*, June 2, 1938, in which the Dean of St. Paul's expresses a similar point of view.
9. John Wheeler-Bennett, *Munich: Prologue to Tragedy*, p. 149; for German text see *Voelkischer Beobachter*, September 27, 1938; for English translation see *Hitler's Speeches, 1922-1939*, translated and edited by Norman H. Baynes (Oxford, 1942), vol. 2, pp. 1487-99.
10. For propaganda reasons Goebbels multiplied the number of German victims by ten when he spoke of 58,000 dead and missing *Volksdeutsche*. Polish

Professor Karol Pospieszalski maintains in his book, *The Case of 58,000 Volksdeutsche*, there were only 2,000 victims to deplore.

11. Their transcripts can be examined and checked in the files of the Armed Forces Investigations Bureau (*Wehrmacht Untersuchungsstelle*) in the German Federal Archives/Military Archives in Freiburg. As to the trustworthiness of the transcripts, see A. de Zayas, "The Wehrmacht Bureau on War Crimes," in *Historical Journal* 35 (1992): 383-399.

12. German Federal Archives-Military Archive (hereafter BA-MA), Record Group RW 2/v.51, p. 32. I spoke with Dr. Schattenberg about this and other cases on October 20, 1975, and further corresponded with him on several different occasions concerning the Bromberg complex 1939.

13. BA-MA, RW 2/v.52, pp. 109-11. I discussed this and other cases with Dr. Boetticher in Munich on April 20, 1976.

14. BA-MA, RW 2/v.56, p. 136. I spoke with Dr. Reger on February 19 and May 10, 1976, about this case and about Reger's extensive hearings conducted in the regions of Posen and Thorn.

15. BA-MA, RW 2/v.56. Concerning the 1939 deportations, an as yet unpublished *Dokumentation der Verschleppungsmaersche* exists in the German Federal Archives, Koblenz, Eastern Documents 7. See also Chapter 15 in A. de Zayas, *The Wehrmacht War Crimes Bureau, 1939-1945* (Lincoln, Neb., 1989), pp. 130-141. For a recent study of the death marches, see Hans Freiherr von Rosen, *Dokumentation der Verschleppung der Deutschen aus Posen—Pommerellen im September 1939* (Berlin, 1990).

16. BA-MA, RW 2/v. 52, pp. 176-77.

17. Wachenheim, "Hitler's Transfers of Population in Eastern Europe," *Foreign Affairs* 20 (1942): 705.

18. 144 B.F.S.P. p. 1072

19. L. Holborn (ed.), *War and Peace Aims of the United Nations*, vol. 1 (New York, 1943), p. 462.

20. International Military Tribunal (IMT), vol. 1, p. 11, emphasis added.

21. Emphasis added. For an interesting overview into the history of the phrase "crimes against humanity," see Schwelb, *Crimes Against Humanity*, 23 B.Y.I.L. (1946), pp 178-226. IMT, vol. 1, p. 11. Also United Nations, *History of the United Nations War Crimes Commission* (London, 1948), especially pp. 35ff and 188ff.

22. IMT, vol. I, p. 63, emphasis added.

23. It became clear that impediments placed in the way of war refugees who wanted to return to their homelands upon cessation of hostilities were, in human rights terms, an equally criminal act.

On December 14, 1945, Captain S. Harris, assistant prosecutor for the United States, introduced evidence in this matter, and read the following excerpt from a report on expulsions from Alsace into the court record: "The first expulsion action was carried out in Alsace in the period from July to December, 1940; in the course of it, 105,000 persons were either expelled or prevented from returning." IMT, Vol. 3, p. 596. Paragraph 11 of UN General Assembly Resolution 194 (III) of December 11, 1948, provides that "the [Palestinian] refugees wishing to return to their homes and live in peace with their neighbors should be permitted to do so at the earliest possible date, and that compensation should be paid for the property of those choosing not to return and for the loss of or damage to property which, under principles of international law or in equity, should be made good by the Governments or authorities responsible."

24. IMT, vol. 2, p.49.
25. IMT, vol. 5, p. 410.
26. IMT, Vol. 6, p. 427.
27. See IMT, vol. 9, p. 312, for Goering's defense, that the Germanization of Poland was carried through only in those regions that had been German before the Versailles Treaty, and that since 1919 the Poles themselves had subjected to similar measures of Polonization—the expulsion of more than one million Germans long settled there.
28. IMT, vol. 3, p. 575.
29. IMT, vol. 8, p. 256.
30. Ibid., p. 253.
31. Ibid.
32. Emphasis added. Joachim von Ribbentrop, Alfred Rosenberg and others were charged with crimes against humanity, found guilty, and hanged on October 16, 1946.
33. IMT, vol. 18, pp. 89-91.
34. IMT, vol. 19, pp. 469.

## Notes to Chapter 3

1. "General Plan-East" was understood as a settlement program for the East ordered by Reichsfuehrer SS Himmler in 1942. See W. Benz, *Die Vertreibung der Deutschen*, pp. 39-48.
2. Translated from the original Russian by A. de Zayas. Original flier at the Politisches Archiv des Auswärtigen Amtes, Bonn, Bestand Völkerrecht/Kriegsrecht, Vol. 82/8. This text is found in a leaflet sent to the German Foreign

Office by its liaison officer Heinrich von zur Mühlen, with whom the author discussed the impact of Ehrenburg's propaganda. See also Ilya Ehrenburg, *Voina* (The War), Vol. 2, pp. 22-23.

3. German Federal Archives/Military Archive (hereafter BA-MA), Bestand H 3/493, Fremde Heere Ost. See also Alexander Werth, *Russia at War* (New York, 1964).

4. Ibid.

5. Ehrenburg, *Russia at War*, pp. 86, 113, 229, 234, 267. See also Militärgeschichtliches Forschungsamt (ed.), *Das Deutsche Reich und der Zweite Weltkrieg*, vol. 4 (Stuttgart, 1983), chapter by Joachim Hoffmann, "Die Kriegführung aus der Sicht der Sowjetunion", pp. 713-809.

6. BA-MA, H 3/493.

7. Order of the Day No. 55, Moscow, 23 February 1942, quoted in J. Stalin, *Ueber den Grossen Vaterländischen Krieg der Sowjetunion* (Berlin, 1951), 2nd ed., pp. 43 et seq.

8. Amberger was a lieutenant of the reserve with the Second Regiment "Hermann Goering," brought in from Memel for the counterattack. His testimony was later submitted by the defence at the Nuremberg trials. The original of the report is found in the German Federal Archives, Koblenz, Ost-Dok. 2, Nr. 13, pp. 9-10.

9. *Le Courrier*, Geneva, 7 November 1944, translated from the French by A. de Zayas.

10. The original of this report is found in the Political Archives of the German Foreign Office in Bonn, Record Group Völkerrecht/Kriegsrecht, vol. 22, Russia, 82/8.

11. Ibid.

12. German Federal Archives, Koblenz, Ost-Dok. 1/31, p. 547.

13. Ost-Dok. 2/20, p. 8.

14. Ost-Dok., 2/14, p. 106.

15. Ost-Dok., 2/9, pp. 309-10.

16. Ost-Dok., 2/8, p. 114.

17. Hans Graf von Lehndorff. *East Prussian Diary, 1945-47* (London, 1963), p. 68. In the years 1975-78, the author visited the late Graf Lehndorff at his residence in Bad Godesberg to discuss his and other testimonies concerning the behavior of the Soviet Army in East Prussia.

18. BA-MA, Record Group H3/1177, pp. 1-4.

19. BA-MA, Record Group H3/665.

20. BA-MA, Record Group H3/1177, pp. 20-21.

21. Aleksandr Solzhenitsyn, *The Gulag Archipelago* (New York, 1974), p. 21.

22. Aleksander Solzhenitsyn, *Prussian Nights: A Poem* (New York, 1977). Translated by Robert Conquest.

23. Lev Kopelev, *No Jail for Thought* (London, 1976).

24. Göttinger Arbeitskreis, *Dokumente der Menschlichkeit* (Würzburg, 1960).

25. Following the publication of the German version of my book *Nemesis at Potsdam* in 1978, Frau Neumann sent me this account, which she had written in 1948. I was so shaken by it that I started a correspondence with her and followed up with two personal visits. Not only was I convinced of the truth of her account but I also learned from her about other abuses, which confirmed the consistent pattern of indiscriminate revenge that befell the entire German civilian population of Eastern Germany. It should also be remembered that Frau Neumann is not the only German woman who had to carry such psychological scars throughout the rest of her life. It is a sad commentary on human nature that, as Frau Neumann confessed to me, no one was interested in her story, no one wanted to listen—all just wanted to forget. Thus, Frau Neumann could not even benefit from the compassion and support that Holocaust survivors received after the war. She, an innocent victim of a brutal war, simply had to carry her sufferings with her, in silence.

26. I met Frau Trakehnen at a conference I delivered in 1980 in Bonn on the expulsion of the Germans. Hers is a private collection of poems, issued without ISBN number. She granted permission to publish it in the German edition of this book. My own English translation is, of course, inferior than the Trakehnen original.

27. George Kennan, *Memoirs, 1925-1950* (Boston, 1967), vol. 1, p. 265.

28. Fritz Brustat-Naval, *Unternehmen Rettung* (Herford, 1970); Christopher Dobson, J. Miller and R. Payne, *The Cruellest Night* (London, 1979); Stephen W. Roskill, *The War at Sea 1939-1945* (London, 1954).

29. Dobson, Miller and Payne, *The Cruellest Night*; Jürgen Rohwer und Gerhard Hümmelchen, *Chronik des Seekrieges 1939-1945* (Oldenbourg, 1968); Cajus Bekker, *Flucht übers Meer* (Oldenbourg, 1959).

30. General Friedrich Hossbach, commander of the Fourth Army and author of the 1937 Hossbach Protocol, which describes how during a general staff conference Hitler outlined his plans for an European war of conquest. I interviewed General Hossbach on several occasions from 1974-77 at his home in Göttingen.

31. Axel Rodenberger, *Der Tod von Dresden* (Frankfurt, 1960), p. 51ff. See also: Max Seydewitz, *Zerstörung und Wiederaufbau von Dresden* (Dresden, 1955); David Irving, *The Destruction of Dresden* (London, 1963).

32. Gerhart Pohl, *Gerhart Hauptmann and Silesia* (Grand Forks, N.D., 1962), p. 8.

33. C.P. Snow, *Science and Government* (Cambridge, Mass., 1961), pp. 47ff; Max Hastings, *Bomber Command* (London, 1979).

## Notes to Chapter 4

1. *United States, Executive Agreement Series* 236, p. 4; *Department of State Bulletin,* V, p. 125; *Documents of American Foreign Relations,* IV, p. 209. Text also in Louise Holborn, *War and Peace Aims of the United Nations,* 1943, p. 2.
2. L. Holborn, *War and Peace Aims of the United Nations,* vol. 2, p. 446.
3. Hubert Ripka, *Munich Before and After* (London, 1939), p. 196. John Wheeler-Bennett, *Munich: Prologue to Tragedy* (London, 1948), p. 155.
4. Arnold Toynbee, *Documents on International Affairs, 1939-46,* vol. 1 (London, 1951), p. 67.
5. Franklin D. Roosevelt Library in Hyde Park, New York, PSF France-Bullitt. With thanks to Dr. Alfred Schickl, Ingolstadt.
6. Radomir Luza, *The Transfer of the Sudeten Germans,* (New York, 1964) p. 236.
7. *Department of State Bulletin,* vol. 11, p. 836, 24 December 1944. *Documents on American Foreign Relations, 1944-45,* vol. 7, p. 898.
8. *Parliamentary Debates, House of Commons,* vol. 406, column 1484.
9. *Foreign Relations of the United States, The Conferences at Malta and Yalta,* p. 509.
10. Ibid., p. 717.
11. Ibid.
12. Ibid., p. 792.
13. Ibid, p. 979.
14. *Foreign Relations of the United States, The Conference of Berlin,* vol. 2, p. 210. Harry Truman, *Memoirs,* vol. 1, p. 369.
15. *Foreign Relations of the United States, The Conference of Berlin,* vol. 2, p. 382.
16. Churchill, *Triumph and Tragedy* (Boston, 1953), p. 658. *Foreign Relations of the United States, The Conference of Berlin,* vol. 2, p. 248.
17. Sir Denis Allen in a letter to the author dated March 15, 1977.
18. Transcript of a conversation with Sir Geoffrey Harrison at his home near London, on October 30, 1976.
19. Conversation with James Riddleberger at his home in Virginia on August 6, 1982.
20. National Archives, Record Group 59, Doc. 740.00119 (Potsdam)/7-2145.
21. *Foreign Relations of the United States, The Conference of Berlin,* vol. 2, p. 1495.
22. Public Record Office, FO 371/46811, Doc. No. C 4415. In 1976 I discussed with Sir Geoffrey Harrison the origin of article 13 and other aspects of his participation at the Potsdam Conference.
23. *Parliamentary Debates, House of Commons,* vol. 397, col. 937.
24. Ibid., vol. 400, col. 784, 24 May 1944.
25. Ibid., vol. 408, col. 1625.

## Notes to Chapter 5

1. *Daily Mail,* August 6, 1945.
2. U.S. Signal Corps, Photo No. SC 334028 of May 8, 1945.
3. *Foreign Relations of the United States, 1945,* vol. 2, pp. 1290-92.
4. Public Record Office, FO 371/47091, Doc. No. N 10436.
5. National Archives, Record Group 85, Box 738, Folder 855—German Population Transfer—Czechoslovakia 1945.
6. Public Record Office, FO 371/46990.
7. "Evacuation and Concentration Camps in Silesia" in *Congressional Record,* Senate, August 2, 1945, Annex A-4778/79.
8. International Committee of the Red Cross, *Report of its Activities during the Second World War* (Geneva, 1948), vol. 1, pp. 334 et seq.
9. Ibid., pp. 675 f.
10. H. G. Adler, *Theresienstadt 1941-1945—Das Antlitz einer Zwangsgemeinschaft* (Tübingen, 1955), p. 214.
11. Alfred Bohmann, *Menschen und Grenzen, Bevoelkerung und Nationalitaeten in Suedosteuropa,* vol. 2 (Cologne, 1969); Gerhard Reichling, *Die deutschen Vertriebenen in Zahlen,* vols 1-2 (Bonn, 1989).
12. For first-hand accounts of this tragedy, see Father Wendelin Gruber, *In the Claws of the Red Dragon,* and Traudie Müller-Wlossak, *The Whip—My Homecoming* (Canberra, Australia, 1982). Both are survivors of the Tito death camps.
13. Theodor Schieder, ed., *Dokumentation der Vertreibung,* vol. 5, p. 92E. Published also in English: *Documents on the Expulsion.*
14. Victor Gollancz, *Our Threatened Values* (London, 1946), p. 96.
15. Letter to the editors of *The Times* (London), October 19, 1945.
16. International Committee of the Red Cross, *Report of the Joint Relief Commission, 1941-1946* (Geneva, 1948), pp. 103-4.
17. *Times* (London), September 10, 1945.
18. National Archives, Record Group 165, Records of the War Department TS OPD Message File, Telegram No. S 28399 of October 18, 1945.
19. Lucius Clay, *Decision in Germany* (New York, 1950), pp. 313-4.
20. Mr. Tischler gave this statement to the author during a meeting in 1985.
21. The original film is in the U.S. Army archives at Tobyhanna, Pennsylvania. A portion of the film was used in a documentary shown on German television in 1981.
22. A German-language version of this film is now in production.
23. The witness is now lives in Düsseldorf.
24. The witness, I.R., now lives in Munich.

25. See also: Landsmannschaft Ostpreussen, ed., *Verschleppt! Frauen und Mädchen von Ostpreussen nach Sibirien verschleppt* (Hamburg, 1978).
26. German Federal Archives, Koblenz, Ost-Dok. 2/9, pp. 622-23.
27. Ost-Dok., 2/20, pp. 109-10.

## Notes to Chapter 6

1. Goethe, *Hermann und Dorothea*, 5th Canto, verses 203-4; 7th Canto, verses 85-90. Translation by Alfred de Zayas.

   Gönnet einander den Platz auf fremdem Boden und teilet,
   Was Ihr habet, zusammen, damit Ihr Barmherzigkeit findet.

   . . . .

   Alle denken gewiss, in kurzen Tagen zur Heimat wieder zu kehren,
   so pflegt sich stets der Vertriebene zu schmeicheln,
   Aber ich täusche mich nicht mit leichter Hoffnung in diesen
   Traurigen Tagen, die uns noch traurige Tage versprechen:
   Denn gelöst sind die Bande der Welt; wer knüpfet sie wieder
   Als allein die Not, die höchste, die uns bevorsteht!

2. The text of this statement was given to the author by Dr. Mende during one of several visits at his residence in Bad Godesberg in 1985.
3. Bund der Vertriebenen (ed.), *Heimat-Freiheit-Menschenrecht* (Bonn, 1976), pp. 14-15. Bund der Vertriebenen, Landesveband Baden-Wuerttemberg, *Drei Jahrzehnte* (Stuttgart, 1975), pp. 17-18.
4. Schiller, *Wilhelm Tell,* Act 4, Scene 2, Verses 2426-2427.
5. Translated by John Koehler.
6. Kulturstiftung der Deutschen Vertriebenen, *Vertrieben . . . Literarische Zeugnisse von Flucht und Vertreibung* (Bonn, 1985).
7. Translation by Alfred de Zayas.
8. Mich rührt so sehr
   böhmischen Volkes Weise
   schleicht sie ins Herz sich leise,
   macht sie es schwer.

   Wenn ein Kind sacht
   singt beim Kartoffeljäten,
   klingt dir sein Leid im späten
   Traum noch der Nacht.

   Magst du auch sein
   weit über Land gefahren,

fällt es dir doch nach Jahren
stets wieder ein.
(Translation by Alfred de Zayas.)

9. Excerpt from Josef von Eichendroff's *Mondnacht*, translation by Alfred de Zayas.

## Notes to Epilogue

1. Albert Schweitzer. *Das Problem des Friedens in der heutigen Welt* (Munich, 1954), p. 6.
2. *Foreign Relations of the United States, 1945*, vol. 2, pp. 1290-91.
3. Department of State, *Bulletin*, vol. 73, September 1, 1975, pp. 304 et seq., at p. 324. See also President Gerald Ford's statement at p. 306.
4. General Assembly Resolution 47/135.

# BIBLIOGRAPHY

Adler, H. G. *Theresienstadt 1941-1945: Das Antlitz einer Zwangsgemeinschaft.* Tübingen, 1955.

Alfredsson, Gudmundur. "Equality and Non-Discrimination: Minority Rights. Report to the Council of Europe in connection with the Seventh International Colloquy on the European Convention on Human Rights, Strasbourg, 1991 [H/Coll (90) 6]. Discussion paper on human rights, fundamental freedoms and the rights of minorities. Submitted to the Third Strasbourg Conference on Parliamentary Democracy, Strasbourg, 1991 [SXB.CONF (III) 8].

Aflredsson, Gudmundur and Alfred de Zayas, "Minority Rights: Protection by the United Nations," *Human Rights Law Journal,* January-February 1993, pp. 1-9.

Andrysek, Oldrich. *Report on the Definition of Minorities.* The Netherlands Institute of Human Rights, SIM Special No. 8, 1989.

Aurich, Peter. *Der deutsch-polnische September 1939.* Munich, 1970.

Bassiouni, Cherif. *Draft Statute International Criminal Tribunal.* Pau, France, 1992.

————. "The Time has come for an International Criminal Court," *Indiana Journal of International and Comparative Law,* vol. 1, 1991, pp. 1 et seq.

Baynes, Norman H. (ed.). *Hitler's Speeches, 1922-1939.* Oxford, 1942.

Bekker, Cajus. *Flucht übers Merr.* Oldenbourg, 1959.

Benes, Eduard. *Memoirs.* London, 1954.

Benz, Wolfgang (ed.). *Die Vertreibung der Deutschen aus dem Osten.* Frankfurt, 1985.

Bergel, Hans. *Die Sachsen in Siebenbuergen.* Innsbruck, 1976.

————. *Siebenbuergen: Bilder einer europäischen Landschaft.* Munich, 1981.

Blumenwitz, Dieter. *Flucht und Vertreibung.* Cologne, 1987.

Boehme, Kurt. *Gesucht Wird*. Munich, 1965.

Bohmann, Alfred. *Die Ausweisung der Sudetendeutschen*. Marburg, 1955.

———. *Menschen und Grenzen*, vols. 1-4, Cologne, 1969-1975.

Born, Joachim, and Dickgiesser, Sylvia. *Deutschsprachige Minderheiten*. Remscheid, 1989.

Bradley, John. *Czechoslovakia: A Short History*. Edinburgh, 1971.

Bramwell, Anna (ed.). *Refugees in the Era of Total War*. London, 1988.

Broszat, Martin. *Zweihundert Jahre deutsche Polenpolitik*. Frankfurt, 1972.

Bruegel, J. W. *Czechoslovakia before Munich*. Cambridge, 1973.

Brustat-Naval, Fritz. *Unternehmen Rettung*. Herford, 1970.

Bund der Vertriebenen. *Der wahre Tatbestand*. Bonn 1960.

———. *Heimat-Freiheit-Menschenrecht*. Bonn, 1976.

———. *Verletzungen von Menschenrechen*. Bonn, 1980.

Bund der Vertriebenen, Landesverband Baden-Württemberg. *Drei Jahrzehnte*. Stuttgart, 1975.

Bundesministerium für Vertriebene. *Zeittafel der Vorgeschichte und des Ablaufs der Vertreibung*, vols. 1-2. Bonn, 1959.

Byrnes, James. *Speaking Frankly*. New York, 1947.

Capotorti, Francesco. *Study on the Rights of Persons Belonging to Ethnic, Religious and Linguistic Minorities*, UN Doc. E/CN.4/Sub.2/384/Rev.1, 1979.

Churchill, Winston. *Closing the Ring*. Boston, 1951

———. *Triumph and Tragedy*. Boston, 1953.

Clay, Lucius. *Decision in Germany*. New York, 1950.

Clemens, Diane. *Yalta*. New York, 1970.

Committee Against Mass Expulsions. *The Land of the Dead*. New York, 1947.

———. *Men Without the Rights of Man*. New York, 1948.

———. *Tragedy of a People*. New York, 1948.

*Congressional Record, United States House of Representatives, United States Senate*, running series, Washington D.C.

Conquest, Robert. *The Great Terror*. London, 1968.

———. *The Soviet Deportation of Nationalities*. London, 1960.

*Courrier de Genève*, November 7, 1944.

Craig, Gordon. *Germany 1886-1945*. Oxford, 1978.

Dallin, Alexander. *German Rule in Russia 1941-45.* London, 1949.

Djilas, Milovan. *Conversations with Stalin.* New York, 1962.

Dobson, Christopher, Miller, J. and Payne, R. *The Cruellest Night.* London, 1979.

*Documents on British Foreign Policy Overseas,* Series 1, vol. 1, London, 1984.

Doenhoff, Marion. *Namen, die keiner mehr nennt.* Munich, 1964.

Drzewieniecki, W. M. *The German Polish Frontier.* Polish Western Association of America, Chicago, 1959.

Dulles, Allen. *Germany Underground.* New York, 1947.

Ehrenburg, Ilya. *Russia at War.* London, 1943.

————. *The War 1941-45.* Cleveland, 1964.

Eisenhower, Dwight D. *Crusade in Europe,* Garden City, 1948.

Ermacora, Felix. *The Protection of Minorities before the United Nations.* Recueil des Cours, vol. 182, pp. 25O et seq., 1983.

Esser, Heinz. *Lamsdorf. Dokumentation über ein polnisches Vernichtungslager.* Bonn, 1971.

Falk, Lucy. *Ich blieb in Königsberg.* Munich, 1965.

Feis, Herbert. *Between War and Peace, The Potsdam Conference,* Princeton, 1960.

————. *Churchill-Roosevelt-Stalin.* Princeton, 1957.

Goldberg, Anatol. *Ilya Ehrenburg, Revolutionary, Novelist, Poet, War Correspondent, Propagandist.* New York, 1984.

Gollancz, Victor. *In Darkest Germany.* London, 1947.

————. *My Dear Timothy.* London, 1952.

————. *Our Threatened Values.* London, 1946.

Goodwin-Gill, Guy. "The Limits of the Power of Expulsion in Public International Law," *British Yearbook of International Law,* vol. 47 (1975), pp. 55-156.

Gordon, Sarah. *Hitler, the Germans and the Jewish Question.* Princeton, 1984.

Göttinger Arbeitskreis/Göttinger Research Committee. *Eastern Germany.* Würzburg, 1961.

————. *Documents of Humanity.* New York: Harper and Brothers, 1954.

Grass, Günter. *Die Blechtrommel,* Frankfurt 1959.

Grau, K. F. *Silesian Inferno.* Cologne, 1970.

Grosser, Alfred. *Germany in Our Time.* London, 1971.

Harris, Arthur. *Bomber Offensive.* London, 1947.

Hastings, Max. *Bomber Command.* London, 1979.

Hilberg, Raul. *The Destruction of the European Jews.* Chicago, 1961.

Hillgruber, Andreas. *Der Zusammenbruch im Osten 1944-45.* Opladen, 1985.

Hoffmann, Joachim, "Die Kriegführung aus der Sicht der Sowjetunion." Militärgeschichtliches Forschungsamt, *Das Deutsche Reich und der Zweite Weltkrieg,* vol. 4, 1983, pp. 713-809.

Hoffmann, Peter. *The History of the German Resistance 1933-1945.* London, 1977.

Holborn, Louise. *War and Peace Aims of the United Nations,* vols. 1- 2. New York, 1943.

Hull, Cordell. *The Memoirs.* London, 1948.

International Committee of the Red Cross. *Report of the International Committee of the Red Cross on its Activities During the Second World War,* vols. 1-3. Geneva, 1948.

————. *Report of the Joint Relief Commission 1941-46,* Geneva, 1948.

International Military Tribunal, *Trial of the Major War Crimnals Before the International Military Tribunal, Nuremberg, 1945-46,* 42 volumes. Nuremberg, 1947-49.

Irving, David. *The Destruction of Dresden.* London, 1963.

Kaps, Johannes. *The Tragedy of Silesia.* Munich, 1952.

Kennan, George. *Memoirs,* vols. 1-2, Boston, 1967, 1972.

Kimminich, Otto. *Das Recht auf die Heimat.* Bonn, 1980.

Koehler, Eve. *Seven Susannahs: Daughters of the Danube.* Milwaukee, 1977.

Kopelev, Lev. *No Jail for Thought.* London, 1976.

Koschyk, Hartmut (ed.). *Das Recht auf die Heimat, Ein Menschenrecht.* Munich, 1992.

Kostrzewski, Joseph. *Poland East of the Oder-Neisse.* London, 1961.

Krockow, Christian Graf von. *Pommern—Bericht aus einem verschwiegenen Land,* Stuttgart, 1985.

————. *Heimat—Erfahrungen mit einem deutschen Thema,* Stuttgart, 1989.

Kruszewsi, Z. Anthony. *The Oder-Neisse Boundary and Poland's Modernization.* New York, 1972.

Krutein, Eva. *Eva's War, A True Story of Survival*. Albuquerque, N.M.: Amador Publishers, 1990.

Kulischer, Eugene. *Europe on the Move*. New York, 1948.

Kulski, W. W. *Germany and Poland*. Syracuse, 1976.

Kulturstiftung der Deutschen Vertriebenen. *Vertrieben . . . Literarische Zeugnisse von Flucht und Vertreibung*. Bonn, 1985.

Kurth, Karl (ed.). *Documents of Humanity*. New York, 1954.

Ladas, Stephen. *The Exchange of Minorities*. New York, 1932.

Landsmannschaft Ostpreussen (ed.). *Verschleppt, Frauen und Mädchen von Ostpreussen nach Sibirien verschleppt*. Hamburg, 1980.

Lane, Arthur Bliss. *I Saw Poland Betrayed. An American Ambassador Reports to the American People*. Indianapolis, 1948.

Leahy, William. *I Was There*. New York, 1950.

Lehmann, Hans Georg. *Der Oder-Neisse Konflikt*. Munich, 1979.

Lehndorff, Hans von. *East Prussian Diary 1945-1947*. London, 1963.

Lemberg, Eugen and F. Edding (eds.). *Die Vertriebenen in Westdeutschland*, vols. 1-3. Kiel, 1959.

Lenz, Siegfried. *Heimatmuseum*, Hamburg: Hoffman und Campe, 1978.

Luza, Radomir. *The Transfer of the Sudeten Germans*. New York, 1964.

Machray, Robert. *East-Prussia: Menace to Poland and Peace*. London, 1943.

————. *The Polish-German Problem*. London, 1941.

Mamatey, Victor, and Luza, Radomir (eds.). *A History of the Czechoslovak Republic 1918-1948*. Princeton, 1973.

Masaryk, Thomas. *The Making of a State*. London, 1927.

————. *The New Europe: The Slav Standpoint*. London, 1918.

————. *The Slavs among the Nations*. London, 1916.

Mee, Charles. *Meeting at Potsdam*. New York, 1975.

Meinecke, Friedrich. *The German Catastrophe*. Boston, 1963.

Mikolajczyk, Stanislaw. *The Pattern of Soviet Domination*. London, 1948.

————. *The Rape of Poland*. New York, 1948.

Militärgeschichtliches Forschungsamt, *Das Deutsche Reich und der Zweite Weltkrieg*, vols. 1-8. Stuttgart, 1978-88.

Morgenthau, Henry. *Germany Is Our Problem*. New York, 1945.

Mueller-Sternberg, Robert. *Deutsche Ostsiedlung—Eine Bilanz fuer Europa.* Bielefeld, 1969.

Mueller-Wlossak, Traudie. *The Whip—My Homecoming.* Canberra, Australia, 1982.

Mullins, Claude. *A Prologue to Nuremberg.* New York, 1982.

Murphy, Robert. *Diplomat Among Warriors.* Garden City, 1964.

Neitmann, Klaus. *Die Staatsvertraege des Deutschen Ordens in Preussen 1230-1449.* Cologne, 1986.

Normann, Käthe von. *Ein Tagebuch aus Pommern 1945-1946.* Munich, 1977.

Paikert, G. C. *The Danube Swabians.* The Hague, 1967.

Palmer, Alan. *The Lands Between: A History of East-Cenral Europe Since the Congress of Vienna.* New York, 1970.

*Parliamentary Debates, House of Commons, House of Lords,* running series, London.

Perman, D. *The Shaping of the Czechoslovak State.* Leiden, 1962.

Permanent Court of International Justice, *Decisions and Judgments,* Series A, B, etc. The Hague, 1919-1939.

Pleyer, Wilhelm. *Dennoch. Neue Gedichte.* Munich, 1953.

Pohl, Gerhart. *Gerhart Hauptmann and Silesia.* Grand Forks, N.D., 1962.

Pospieszalski, Karol. *The Case of 58,000 Volksdeutsche.* Documenta Occupationis, Instytut Zachodni, vol. 7. Poznan, 1959.

Price, Harry. *The Marshall Plan and Its Meaning.* Ithaca, 1955.

Proudfoot, Malcolm. *European Refugees: 1939-1952. A Study in Forced Population Movement.* London, 1957.

Rauschning, Hermann. *Die Entdeutschung Posens und Westpreussens.* Berlin, 1930.

Reichling, Gerhard. *Die deutschen Vertriebenen in Zahlen,* vols. 1-2. Bonn, 1989.

Rhode, Gotthold. *Kleine Geschichte Polens.* Darmstadt, 1965.

Ripka, Hubert. *The Future of the Czechoslovak Germans.* London, 1944.

———. *Munich: Before and After.* London, 1939.

Rodenberger, Axel. *Der Tod von Dresden.* Frankfurt, 1960.

Rohwer, Jürgen and Gerhard Hümmelchen. *Chronik des Seekrieges 1939-1945.* Oldenbourg, 1968.

Rosen, Hans Freiherr von. *Dokumentation der Verschleppung der Deutschen aus Posen-Pommerellen im September 1939,* Berlin: Westkreuz Verlag, 1990.

Roskill, Stephen W. *The War at Sea, 1939-1945.* London, 1954.

Rothfels, Hans. *German Opposition to Hitler.* London, 1961.

Schechtman, Joseph. *European Population Transfers.* New York, 1946.

————. "The Elimination of German Minorities in Southeastern Europe," *Journal of Central European Affairs,* July 1946, pp. 160 et seq.

————."Postwar Population Transfers in Europe," *Review of Politics,* vol. 15, 1953, pp. 151 et seq.

Schieder, Theodor (ed.). *Documents of the Expulsion of the Germans,* vols. 1-8. Bonn, 1958-1961.

Schimitzek, Stanislav. *Truth or Conjecture: German Civilian Losses in the East.* Warsaw, 1966.

Schoen, Heinz. *Ostsee '45.* Stuttgart, 1983.

Schoenberg, Hans. *Germans from the East.* The Hague, 1970.

Schulz, Eberhard (ed.). *Leistung und Schicksal.* Cologne, 1967.

Schwarz, Leo. *Refugees in Germany Today.* New York, 1957.

Schweitzer, Albert. *Das Problem des Friedens in der heutigen Welt.* Munich, 1954.

Schweizerisches Rotes Kreuz. *Das Schweizerische Rote Kreuz - Eine Sondernummer des deutschen Fluechtlingsproblems,* No. 11/12. Bern, 1949.

————. *Volk ohne Raum—Berichte aus deutscen Flüchtlingslagern.* Bern, 1949.

Schwelb, E. "Crimes Against Humanity," *British Yearbook of International Law* (1946), pp. 178-226.

Selle, Götz von. *Ostdeutsche Biographien.* Wuerzburg, 1955.

Seydewitz, Max. *Zerstoerung und Wiederaufbau von Dresden.* Dresden, 1955.

Shelton, Regina. *To Lose a War.* Carbondale, Ill., 1980.

Sherwood, R. E. *Roosevelt and Hopkins: An Intimate History.* New York, 1948.

————. *The White House Papers of Harry L. Hopkins.* London, 1948-9.

Skubiszewski, Karol. "Le Transfert de la population allemande, était-il conforme au droit international?" *Cahiers Pologne-Allemagne* (1959), p. 42 et seq.

Snow, C. P. *Science and Government.* Cambridge, Mass, 1961.

Solzhenitsin, Alexander. *The Gulag Archipelago.* New York, 1974.

————. *Prussian Nights: A Poem.* Translated by Robert Conquest. New York, 1977.

Stalin, Joseph. *Ueber den Grossen Vaterländischen Krieg der Sowjetunion,* 2nd edition. East Berlin, 1951.

Statistisches Bundesamt. *Die deutschen Vertreibungsverluste.* Wiesbaden, 1958.

Stump, Karl. *The German-Russians: Two Centuries of Pioneering.* Bonn, 1967.

Surminski, Arno. *Jokehnen. Oder wie lange fährt man von Ostpreussen nach Deutschland?* Hamburg: Hoffmann und Campe, 1974.

————. *Kudenow. Oder An fremden Wassern weinen.* Hamburg: Hoffmann und Campe, 1978.

Taborsky, Eduard. *Benes and Stalin.* Moscow, 1943, 1945; Springfield, Ill., 1954.

————. *The Czechoslovak Cause.* London, 1944.

————. *Czechoslovak Democracy at Work.* London, 1945.

Thompson, Laurence. *The Greatest Treason.* New York, 1968.

Thornberry, Patrick. *International Law and the Rights of Minorities.* Oxford, 1991.

Tomuschat, Christian. "Protection of Minorities under Article 27 of the International Covenant on Civil and Political Rights," in *Voelkerrecht als Rechtsordnung, Internationale Gerichtsbarkeit, Menschenrechte, Festschrift für Hermann Mosler.* Cologne, 1983, pp. 949-979.

Toynbee, Arnold. *Documents on International Affairs, 1939-46,* vol. 1, London, 1951.

————. *The World After the Peace Conference.* London, 1926.

————. "A Turning Point in History," *Foreign Affairs* (January 1939), p. 316.

Truhardt, Herbert von. *Völkerbund und Minderheitenpetitionen.* Leipzig, 1931.

Truman, Harry. *Memoirs,* vols. 1-2. New York, 1955.

United Nations, *History of the United Nations War Crimes Commission.* London, 1948.

United States Department of State. *Foreign Relations of the United States, the Conferences at Malta and Yalta, 1945; The Conference at Berlin, 1945:* vols. 1-2; *General, Political and Economic Matters,* 1945, vol. 2.

————. *Papers Relating to the Foreign Relations of the United States, the Paris Peace Conference, 1919,* vols. 1-12.

Vetter, Roland. *Herz der Batschka—Tscherwenka.* Mannheim, 1976.

Vorbach, Walter. *Geliebtes Leben. Gedichte.* Nuremberg, 1987.

Wachenheim, "Hitler's Transfers of Population in Eastern Europe," *Foreign Affairs,* vol. 20, 1942, pp. 707 et seq.

Wagner, Wolfgang. *The Genesis of the Oder-Neisse Line.* Stuttgart, 1957.

Wambaugh, Sarah. *Plebiscites since the World War.* Washington, 1933.

Weidenfeld, Werner (ed.). *Handwörterbuch zur Deutschen Einheit.* Frankfurt, 1992.

Welles, Sumner. *The Time for Decision.* New York, 1944.

Werth, Alexander. *Russia at War 1941-1945.* New York, 1964.

Wheeler-Bennett, John. *Munich, Prologue to Tragedy.* New York, 1948.

Wild, Georg (ed.). *Franz Hamm zum 80. Geburtstag.* Munich, 1980.

Wiewiora, Boleslav. *The Polish-German Frontier.* Poznan, 1964.

Winiewicz, Jozef. *The Polish-German Frontier.* London, 1944.

Wiskemann, Elisabeth. *Czechs and Germans.* New York, 1967.

———. *Germany's Eastern Neighbours.* London, 1956.

———. *Undeclared War,* London, 1967.

Zayas, Alfred-Maurice de. *Nemesis at Potsdam,* 3rd edition. Lincoln, Neb., 1990.

———. *The Wehrmacht War Crimes Bureau,* 2nd edition. Lincoln, Neb., 1990.

———. "The International Judicial Protection of Minority Rights," in C. Brölmann, R. Lefeber and M. Zieck (eds.), *Peoples and Minorities in International Law.* Amsterdam, 1993.

———. "International Law and Mass Population Transfers," *Harvard International Law Journal,* vol. 16 (1975), pp. 207-58.

———. "The Legality of Mass Population Transfers: The German Experience 1945-48," *East European Quarterly,* vol. XII, nos. 1-2 (1978), pp. 1-23 and 144-160.

———. "Twentieth Century Expulsions" in Anna Bramwell (ed.), *Refugees in the Era of Total War.* London, 1988, pp. 15-38.

———. "The Wehrmacht Bureau on War Crimes," *Historical Journal,* vol. 35 (1992), pp. 383-399.

———. Various entries in R. Bernhardt, *Encyclopedia of Public Inernational Law.* Amsterdam, 1981-1989: " Amnesty Clause"; "Civilian Population, Protection"; "Combatants"; "Curzon Line"; "European Recovery Program (Marshall Plan)"; "Forced Resettlement"; "Open Towns"; "Peace of Westphalia"; "Population, Expulsion and Transfer"; "Repatriation"; "Territory, Abandonment"; "United Nations Relief and Rehabilitation Activities."

# INDEX